Problem Booklet

To Accompany
Accounting, 19e

OR

Financial Accounting, 7e

For use with General Ledger Software

Prepared by

Dale Klooster
Educational Technical Systems

Warren Allen
Educational Technical Systems

South-Western College Publishing
an International Thomson Publishing company I T P®

Cincinnati • Albany • Boston • Detroit • Johannesburg • London • Madrid • Melbourne • Mexico City
New York • Pacific Grove • San Francisco • Scottsdale • Singapore • Tokyo • Toronto

Accounting Team Director: Richard Lindgren
Senior Acquisitions Editor: David L. Shaut
Senior Marketing Manager: Sharon Oblinger
Senior Developmental Editor: Ken Martin
Production Editor: Mark Sears
Media Production Editor: Lora Craver
Production Services: Laurie Merz

International Thomson Publishing
South-Western is an ITP Company. The ITP trademark is used under license.

ISBN: 0-538-87425-2

6 7 GP 4 3 2 1 0

Printed in the United States of America

TABLE OF CONTENTS

Student Reference Guide:

GENERAL LEDGER SOFTWARE PROBLEMS
AND
STEP-BY-STEP PROBLEM INSTRUCTIONS

DOS Start-Up Instructions

Use the following steps to start up the General Ledger Software

1. Start your computer.
2. At the DOS prompt, place your program disk in the disk drive.
3. Enter IA1 to load the program in the computer memory.

Windows Installation Instructions

Use the following steps to install the General Ledger Software.

1. Choose **Run** from the File menu of Program Manager and key **a:setup** in the command line.
2. To start-up General Ledger Software, double-click on the **General Ledger Software** icon or choose **General Ledger Software** from the Start button.

Problem 2–2A
Journal entries and trial balance
Objectives 2, 3, 4, 5

On October 1 of the current year, Clay Bryant established Northside Realty, which completed the following transactions during the month:
   a. Clay Bryant transferred cash from a personal bank account to an account to be used for the business, $25,000.
   b. Purchased supplies on account, $2,900.
   c. Earned sales commissions, receiving cash, $32,600.
   d. Paid rent on office and equipment for the month, $4,500.
   e. Paid creditor on account, $1,000.
   f. Withdrew cash for personal use, $2,000.
   g. Paid automobile expenses (including rental charge) for month, $1,900, and miscellaneous expenses, $1,050.
   h. Paid office salaries, $4,000.
   i. Determined that the cost of supplies used was $1,250.

Instructions

1. Journalze entries for transactions (a) through (i), using the following account titles: Cash; Supplies; Accounts Payable; Clay Bryant, Capital; Clay Bryant, Drawing; Sales Commissions; Rent Expense; Office Salaries Expense; Automobile Expense; Supplies Expense; Miscellaneous Expense. Journal entry explanations may be omitted.
2. Prepare T accounts, using the account titles in (1). Post the journal entries to these accounts, placing the appropriate letter to the left of each amount to identify the transactions. Determine the account balances, after all posting is complete, for all accounts having two or more debits or credits. A memorandum balance should be inserted in accounts having both debits and credits, in the manner illustrated in the chapter. For accounts with entries on one side only, there is no need to insert a memorandum balance in the item column. For accounts containing only a single debit and a single credit, the memorandum balance should be inserted in the appropriate item column.
3. Prepare a trial balance as of October 31, 20—.
4. Determine the following:
   a. Amount of total revenue recorded in the ledger.
   b. Amount of total expenses recorded in the ledger.
   c. Amount of net income for October.

DOS Instructions

1. Load the General Ledger Software program (IA1) from the program disk.

   Key **IA1** and press Enter at the DOS prompt. To the question "Read About General Ledger Software?" select **No** to bypass the copyright screens.

2. Load the file **02-2A** from the program disk.

   Press the **Alt** key to activate menu selection. Choose the **Open Accounting File** command in the File menu. Select the **Files** button and choose the accounting file to open. Select the Ok button to open the file.

3. Carefully key your name in the Student Name field in the General Information window. Press Ctrl+Enter to select Ok.

4. Choose the **Save As** command in the File menu and save the file to the drive and directory containing your data files. Key a file name of XXX2-2A (where XXX are your initials). Press Ctrl+Enter to select Ok.

5. Key the journal entries in the General Journal.

   Type the current year and enter 10/31 as the date for each transaction. Key the letter for each entry in the Reference field; for example, (a), (b), etc. To display a list of accounts, press the F1 key. After each journal entry is keyed, press Ctrl+Enter to select Ok. When the Posting Summary window appears, press Ctrl+Enter to Post.

6. Display the journal entries.

   Select **Journals** from the Reports menu and select **General Journal** in the Report Selection window. Select the Ok button in the Selection Options window to display the journal entries for 10/31/--. Press the F9 key to print the general journal report.

7. Make corrections to the journal entries, if necessary.

   Select **List** in the General Journal window to display the journal entries. Select the entry for correction and make the necessary change(s).

8. Display a trial balance.

   Select **Ledgers** from the Reports menu and select **Trial Balance** in the Report Selection window. Press the F9 key to print the trial balance report.

9. Display the income statement, balance sheet, and statement of owner's equity.

   Select **Financial Statements** from the Reports menu and select **Income Statement, Balance Sheet,** and **Statement of Owner's Equity** in the Report Selection window. Press the F9 key to print each report.

10. Choose the **Save Accounting File** command in the File menu to save your data file.

Windows Instructions

To access Help, click on the Help button that appears in most windows.

1. Click on the **Open** toolbar button and double-click on 02-2A to open the file.

2. Carefully key your name in the User Name field and click on the OK button.

3. Click on the **Save As** toolbar button and save the file to the drive and directory containing your data files. Key a file name of XXX2-2A (where XXX are your initials). Click on the OK button.

4. Click on the **Journal** toolbar button and key the journal entries in the General Journal.

   Key 10/31/-- (where -- is the current year) as the date for each transaction. Key the letter for each entry in the Reference field: for example, (a), (b), etc. After each journal entry is keyed, click on the **Post** button (or press Enter).

5. Display the journal entries.

   Click on the **Reports** toolbar button and click on **Journals** in the Report Selection window. Click on **General Journal** and the OK button to choose a report to display. Click on **Include All Journal Entries** and the OK button to display the general journal report. To print the report, click on the **Print** button.

6. Make corrections to the journal entries, if necessary.

   In the General Journal window, click on the entry to correct, then key the correction(s) to the journal entry and click on the **Post** button (or press Enter).

7. Display the trial balance.

   Click on the **Reports** toolbar button and click on **Ledger Reports**. Click on **Trial Balance** and the OK button to choose a report to display. To print the report, click on the **Print** button.

8. Display the income statement, balance sheet, and statement of owner's equity.

Click on the **Reports** toolbar button and click on **Financial Statements**. Click on **Income Statement, Balance Sheet**, and **Statement of Owner's Equity**. To print each report, click on the **Print** button.

9. Click on the **Save** toolbar button to save your data file.

Problem 2–3A
Journal entries and trial balance
Objectives 2, 3, 4, 5

On July 10 of the current year, Jong Woo established an interior decorating business, Asian Designs. During the remainder of the month, Jong Woo completed the following transactions related to the business:

July 10. Jong transferred cash from a personal bank account to an account to be used for the business, $20,000.
10. Paid rent for period of July 10 to end of month, $1,500.
11. Purchased a truck for $15,000, paying $5,000 cash and giving a note payable for the remainder.
12. Purchased equipment on account, $2,500.
14. Purchased supplies for cash, $1,050.
14. Paid premiums on property and casualty insurance, $750.
15. Received cash for job completed, $3,100.
21. Paid creditor for equipment purchased on July 12, $2,500.
24. Recorded jobs completed on account and sent invoices to customers, $3,100.
26. Received an invoice for truck expenses, to be paid in August, $225.
27. Paid utilities expense, $1,205.
27. Paid miscellaneous expenses, $173.
28. Received cash from customers on account, $1,420.
31. Paid wages of employees, $2,100.
31. Withdrew cash for personal use, $1,500.

Instructions

1. Journalize each transaction in a two-column journal, referring to the following chart of accounts in selecting the accounts to be debited and credited. (Do not insert the account numbers in the journal at this time.) Journal entry explanations may be omitted.

11	Cash	31	Jong Woo, Capital
12	Accounts Receivable	32	Jong Woo, Drawing
13	Supplies	41	Fees Earned= *EARNED REVENUE*
14	Prepaid Insurance	51	Wages Expense
16	Equipment	53	Rent Expense
18	Truck	54	Utilities Expense
21	Notes Payable	55	Truck Expense
22	Accounts Payable	59	Miscellaneous Expense

2. Post the journal to a ledger of four-column accounts, inserting appropriate posting references as each item is posted. Extend the balances to the appropriate balance columns after each transaction is posted.
3. Prepare a trial balance for Asian Designs as of July 31.

DOS Instructions

1. Load the General Ledger Software program (IA1) from the program disk.

   Key **IA1** and press Enter at the DOS prompt. To the question "Read About General Ledger Software?" select **No** to bypass the copyright screens.

2. Load the file **02-3A** from the program disk.

   Press the **Alt** key to activate menu selection. Choose the **Open Accounting File** command in the File menu. Select the **Files** button and choose the accounting file to open. Select the Ok button to open the file.

3. Carefully key your name in the Student Name field in the General Information window. Press Ctrl+Enter to select Ok.

4. Choose the **Save As** command in the File menu and save the file to the drive and directory containing your data files. Key a file name of XXX2-3A (where XXX are your initials). Press Ctrl+Enter to select Ok.

5. Key the journal entries in the General Journal.

   Key the date for each transaction. Leave the Reference field blank. After each journal entry is keyed, press Ctrl+Enter to select Ok. When the Posting Summary window appears, press Ctrl+Enter to Post.

6. Display the journal entries.

   Select **Journals** from the Reports menu and select **General Journal** in the Report Selection window. Select the Ok button in the Selection Options window to display the journal entries for July. Press the F9 key to print the general journal report.

7. Make corrections to the journal entries, if necessary.

   Select **List** in the General Journal window to display the journal entries. Select the entry for correction and make the necessary change(s).

8. Display a trial balance.

   Select **Ledgers** from the Reports menu and select **Trial Balance** in the Report Selection window. Press the F9 key to print the trial balance report.

9. Display the income statement, balance sheet, and statement of owner's equity.

   Select **Financial Statements** from the Reports menu and select **Income Statement, Balance Sheet,** and **Statement of Owner's Equity** in the Report Selection window. Press the F9 key to print each report.

10. Choose the **Save Accounting File** command in the File menu to save your data file.

Windows Instructions

To access Help, click on the Help button that appears in most windows.

1. Click on the **Open** toolbar button and double-click on 02-3A to open the file.

2. Carefully key your name in the User Name field and click on the OK button.

3. Click on the **Save As** toolbar button and save the file to the drive and directory containing your data files. Key a file name of XXX2-3A (where XXX are your initials). Click on the OK button.

4. Click on the **Journal** toolbar button and key the journal entries in the General Journal.

   Key the date for each transaction. Leave the Reference field blank. After each journal entry is keyed, click on the **Post** button (or press Enter).

5. Display the journal entries.

   Click on the **Reports** toolbar button and click on **Journals** in the Report Selection window. Click on **General Journal** and the OK button to choose a report to display. Click on **Include All Journal Entries** and the OK button to display the general journal report. To print the report, click on the **Print** button.

6. Make corrections to the journal entries, if necessary.

   In the General Journal window, click on the entry to correct, then key the correction(s) to the journal entry and click on the **Post** button (or press Enter).

7. Display the trial balance.

   Click on the **Reports** toolbar button and click on **Ledger Reports**. Click on **Trial Balance** and the OK button to choose a report to display. To print the report, click on the **Print** button.

8. Display the income statement, balance sheet, and statement of owner's equity.

   Click on the **Reports** toolbar button and click on Financial Statements. Click on **Income Statement, Balance Sheet,** and **Statement of Owner's Equity**. To print each report, click on the **Print** button.

9. Click on the **Save** toolbar button to save your data file.

Problem 2–2B
Journal entries and trial balance
Objectives 2, 3, 4, 5

On July 1 of the current year, Lamar Todd established Sky Realty, which completed the following transactions during the month:

a. Lamar Todd transferred cash from a personal bank account to an account to be used for the business, $15,000.
b. Paid rent on office and equipment for the month, $2,500.
c. Purchased supplies on account, $1,500.
d. Paid creditor on account, $900.
e. Earned sales commissions, receiving cash, $20,750.
f. Paid automobile expenses (including rental charge) for month, $2,400, and miscellaneous expenses, $1,250.
g. Paid office salaries, $4,000.
h. Determined that the cost of supplies used was $1,050.
i. Withdrew cash for personal use, $1,500.

Instructions

1. Journalize entries for transactions (a) through (i), using the following account titles: Cash; Supplies; Accounts Payable; Lamar Todd, Capital; Lamar Todd, Drawing; Sales Commissions; Office Salaries Expense; Rent Expense; Automobile Expense; Supplies Expense; Miscellaneous Expense. Explanations may be omitted.
2. Prepare T accounts, using the account titles in (1). Post the journal entries to these accounts, placing the appropriate letter to the left of each amount to identify the transactions. Determine the account balances, after all posting is complete, for all accounts having two or more debits or credits. A memorandum balance should also be inserted in accounts having both debits and credits, in the manner illustrated in the chapter. For accounts with entries on one side only, there is no need to insert a memorandum balance in the item column. For accounts containing only a single debit and a single credit, the memorandum balance should be inserted in the appropriate item column.
3. Prepare a trial balance as of July 31, 19—.
4. Determine the following:
   a. Amount of total revenue recorded in the ledger.
   b. Amount of total expenses recorded in the ledger.
   c. Amount of net income for July.

DOS Instructions

1. Load the General Ledger Software program (IA1) from the program disk.

   Key **IA1** and press Enter at the DOS prompt. To the question "Read About General Ledger Software?" select **No** to bypass the copyright screens.

2. Load the file **02-2B** from the program disk.

   Press the **Alt** key to activate menu selection. Choose the **Open Accounting File** command in the File menu. Select the **Files** button and choose the accounting file to open. Select the Ok button to open the file.

3. Carefully key your name in the Student Name field in the General Information window. Press Ctrl+Enter to select Ok.

4. Choose the **Save As** command in the File menu and save the file to the drive and directory containing your data files. Key a file name of XXX2-2B (where XXX are your initials). Press Ctrl+Enter to select Ok.

5. Key the journal entries in the General Journal.

   Type the current year and enter 07/31 as the date for each transaction. Key the letter for each entry in the Reference field; for example, (a), (b), etc. To display a list of accounts, press the F1 key. After each journal entry is keyed, press Ctrl+Enter to select Ok. When the Posting Summary window appears, press Ctrl+Enter to Post.

6. Display the journal entries.

   Select **Journals** from the Reports menu and select **General Journal** in the Report Selection window. Select the Ok button in the Selection Options window to display the journal entries for 07/31/--. Press the F9 key to print the general journal report.

7. Make corrections to the journal entries, if necessary.

Select **List** in the General Journal window to display the journal entries. Select the entry for correction and make the necessary change(s).

8. Display a trial balance.

   Select **Ledgers** from the Reports menu and select **Trial Balance** in the Report Selection window. Press the F9 key to print the trial balance report.

9. Display the income statement, balance sheet, and statement of owner's equity.

   Select **Financial Statements** from the Reports menu and select **Income Statement, Balance Sheet,** and **Statement of Owner's Equity** in the Report Selection window. Press the F9 key to print each report.

10. Choose the **Save Accounting File** command in the File menu to save your data file.

Windows Instructions

To access Help, click on the Help button that appears in most windows.

1. Click on the **Open** toolbar button and double-click on 02-2B to open the file.

2. Carefully key your name in the User Name field and click on the OK button.

3. Click on the **Save As** toolbar button and save the file to the drive and directory containing your data files. Key a file name of XXX2-2B (where XXX are your initials). Click on the OK button.

4. Click on the **Journal** toolbar button and key the journal entries in the General Journal.

   Key 07/31/-- (where -- is the current year) as the date for each transaction. Key the letter for each entry in the Reference field: for example, (a), (b), etc. After each journal entry is keyed, click on the **Post** button (or press Enter).

5. Display the journal entries.

   Click on the **Reports** toolbar button and click on **Journals** in the Report Selection window. Click on **General Journal** and the OK button to choose a report to display. Click on **Include All Journal Entries** and the OK button to display the general journal report. To print the report, click on the **Print** button.

6. Make corrections to the journal entries, if necessary.

   In the General Journal window, click on the entry to correct, then key the correction(s) to the journal entry and click on the **Post** button (or press Enter).

7. Display the trial balance.

   Click on the **Reports** toolbar button and click on **Ledger Reports**. Click on **Trial Balance** and the OK button to choose a report to display. To print the report, click on the **Print** button.

8. Display the income statement, balance sheet, and statement of owner's equity.

   Click on the **Reports** toolbar button and click on **Financial Statements**. Click on **Income Statement, Balance Sheet,** and **Statement of Owner's Equity**. To print each report, click on the **Print** button.

9. Click on the **Save** toolbar button to save your data file.

Problem 2–3B
Journal entries and trial balance
Objectives 2, 3, 4, 5

On June 5 of the current year, Dave Chapman established an interior decorating business, Modern Designs. During the remainder of the month, Dave completed the following transactions related to the business:

June   5. Dave transferred cash from a personal bank account to an account to be used for the business, $25,000.

         5. Paid rent for period of June 5 to end of month, $1,700.

         7. Purchased office equipment on account, $10,500.

         8. Purchased a used truck for $18,000, paying $10,000 cash and giving a note payable for the remainder.

       10. Purchased supplies for cash, $1,315.

       12. Received cash for job completed, $3,300.

       20. Paid premiums on property and casualty insurance, $800.

June   22. Recorded jobs completed on account and sent invoices to customers, $1,950.
      24. Received an invoice for truck expenses, to be paid in July, $290.
      29. Paid utilities expense, $490.
      29. Paid miscellaneous expenses, $195.
      30. Received cash from customers on account, $1,200.
      30. Paid wages of employees, $1,900.
      30. Paid creditor a portion of the amount owed for equipment purchased on June 7, $3,000.
      30. Withdrew cash for personal use, $2,500.

Instructions

1. Journalize each transaction in a two-column journal, referring to the following chart of accounts in selecting the accounts to be debited and credited. (Do not insert the account numbers in the journal at this time.) Explanations may be omitted.

11	Cash	31	Dave Chapman, Capital
12	Accounts Receivable	32	Dave Chapman, Drawing
13	Supplies	41	Fees Earned
14	Prepaid Insurance	51	Wages Expense
16	Equipment	53	Rent Expense
18	Truck	54	Utilities Expense
21	Notes Payable	55	Truck Expense
22	Accounts Payable	59	Miscellaneous Expense

2. Post the journal to a ledger of four-column accounts, inserting appropriate posting references as each item is posted. Extend the balances to the appropriate balance columns after each transaction is posted.
3. Prepare a trial balance for Modern Designs as of June 30.

DOS Instructions

1. Load the General Ledger Software program (IA1) from the program disk.

   Key **IA1** and press Enter at the DOS prompt. To the question "Read About General Ledger Software?" select **No** to bypass the copyright screens.

2. Load the file **02-3B** from the program disk.

   Press the **Alt** key to activate menu selection. Choose the **Open Accounting File** command in the File menu. Select the **Files** button and choose the accounting file to open. Select the Ok button to open the file.

3. Carefully key your name in the Student Name field in the General Information window. Press Ctrl+Enter to select Ok.

4. Choose the **Save As** command in the File menu and save the file to the drive and directory containing your data files. Key a file name of XXX2-3B (where XXX are your initials). Press Ctrl+Enter to select Ok.

5. Key the journal entries in the General Journal.

   Key the date for each transaction. Leave the Reference field blank. After each journal entry is keyed, press Ctrl+Enter to select Ok. When the Posting Summary window appears, press Ctrl+Enter to Post.

6. Display the journal entries.

   Select **Journals** from the Reports menu and select **General Journal** in the Report Selection window. Select the Ok button in the Selection Options window to display the journal entries for June. Press the F9 key to print the general journal report.

7. Make corrections to the journal entries, if necessary.

   Select **List** in the General Journal window to display the journal entries. Select the entry for correction and make the necessary change(s).

8. Display a trial balance.

   Select **Ledgers** from the Reports menu and select **Trial Balance** in the Report Selection window. Press the F9 key to print the trial balance report.

9. Display the income statement, balance sheet, and statement of owner's equity.

   Select **Financial Statements** from the Reports menu and select **Income Statement, Balance Sheet,** and **Statement of Owner's Equity** in the Report Selection window. Press the F9 key to print each report.

10. Choose the **Save Accounting File** command in the File menu to save your data file.

Windows Instructions

To access Help, click on the Help button that appears in most windows.

1. Click on the **Open** toolbar button and double-click on 02-3B to open the file.

2. Carefully key your name in the User Name field and click on the OK button.

3. Click on the **Save As** toolbar button and save the file to the drive and directory containing your data files. Key a file name of XXX2-3B (where XXX are your initials). Click on the OK button.

4. Click on the **Journal** toolbar button and key the journal entries in the General Journal.

   Key the date for each transaction. Leave the Reference field blank. After each journal entry is keyed, click on the **Post** button (or press Enter).

5. Display the journal entries.

   Click on the **Reports** toolbar button and click on **Journals** in the Report Selection window. Click on **General Journal** and the OK button to choose a report to display. Click on **Include All Journal Entries** and the OK button to display the general journal report. To print the report, click on the **Print** button.

6. Make corrections to the journal entries, if necessary.

   In the General Journal window, click on the entry to correct, then key the correction(s) to the journal entry and click on the **Post** button (or press Enter).

7. Display the trial balance.

   Click on the **Reports** toolbar button and click on **Ledger Reports.** Click on **Trial Balance** and the OK button to choose a report to display. To print the report, click on the **Print** button.

8. Display the income statement, balance sheet, and statement of owner's equity.

   Click on the **Reports** toolbar button and click on **Financial Statements.** Click on **Income Statement, Balance Sheet,** and **Statement of Owner's Equity.** To print each report, click on the **Print** button.

9. Click on the **Save** toolbar button to save your data file.

Problem 3–4A
Adjusting Entries
Objective 3

Rainbow Trout Co., an outfitter store for fishing treks, prepared the following trial balance at the end of its first year of operations:

Rainbow Trout Co.
Trial Balance
April 30, 20—

Cash..	1,150	
Accounts Receivable...	3,500	
Supplies	1,300	
Equipment..	9,900	
Accounts Payable		750
Unearned Fees		2,000
Lee Wulff, Capital...		10,500
Lee Wulff, Drawing...	1,000	
Fees Earned...		36,750
Wages Expense..	19,500	
Rent Expense..	9,000	
Utilities Expense...	3,750	
Miscellaneous Expense	900	
	50,000	50,000

For preparing the adjusting entries, the following data were assembled:

a. Supplies on hand on April 30 were $175.
b. Fees earned but unbilled on April 30 were $1,380.
c. Depreciation of equipment was estimated to be $800 for the year.
d. Unpaid wages accrued on April 30 were $450.
e. The balance in unearned fees represented the Jan. 1 receipt in advance for services to be provided. Only $750 of the services were provided between Jan. 1 and April 30.

Instructions

Journalize the adjusting entries necessary on April 30.

DOS Instructions

1. Load the General Ledger Software program (IA1) from the program disk.

   Key **IA1** and press Enter at the DOS prompt. To the question "Read About General Ledger Software?" select **No** to bypass the copyright screens.

2. Load the file **03-4A** from the program disk.

   Press the **Alt** key to activate menu selection. Choose the **Open Accounting File** command in the File menu. Select the **Files** button and choose the accounting file to open. Select the Ok button to open the file.

3. Carefully key your name in the Student Name field in the General Information window. Press Ctrl+Enter to select Ok.

4. Choose the **Save As** command in the File menu and save the file to the drive and directory containing your data files. Key a file name of XXX3-4A (where XXX are your initials). Press Ctrl+Enter to select Ok.

5. Key the adjusting entries in the General Journal.

   Type the current year and enter 04/30 as the date for each entry. Key the letter for each adjusting entry in the Reference field; for example, (a), (b), etc. To display a list of accounts, press the F1 key. After each entry is keyed, press Ctrl+Enter to select Ok. When the Posting Summary window appears, press Ctrl+Enter to Post.

6. Display the adjusting entries.

   Select **Journals** from the Reports menu and select **General Journal** in the Report Selection window. Select the Ok button in the Selection Options window to display the adjusting entries. Press the F9 key to print the general journal report.

7. Make corrections to the adjusting entries, if necessary.

   Select **List** in the General Journal window to display the adjusting entries. Select the entry for correction and make the necessary change(s).

8. Display the income statement, balance sheet, and statement of owner's equity.

   Select **Financial Statements** from the Reports menu and select **Income Statement, Balance Sheet,** and **Statement of Owner's Equity** in the Report Selection window. Press the F9 key to print each report.

9. Choose the **Save Accounting File** command in the File menu to save your data file.

Windows Instructions

To access Help, click on the Help button that appears in most windows.

1. Click on the **Open** toolbar button and double-click on 03-4A to open the file.

2. Carefully key your name in the User Name field and click on the OK button.

3. Click on the **Save As** toolbar button and save the file to the drive and directory containing your data files. Key a file name of XXX3-4A (where XXX are your initials). Click on the OK button.

4. Click on the **Journal** toolbar button and key the adjusting entries in the General Journal.

Key 04/30/-- (where -- is the current year) as the date for each entry. Key the letter for each adjusting entry in the Reference field; for example, (a), (b), etc. After each entry is keyed, click on the **Post** button (or press Enter).

5. Display the adjusting entries.

   Click on the **Reports** toolbar button and click on **Journals** in the Report Selection window. Click on **General Journal** and the OK button to choose a report to display. Click on **Include All Journal Entries** and the OK button to display the adjusting entries report. To print the report, click on the **Print** button.

6. Make corrections to the adjusting entries, if necessary.

   In the General Journal window, click on the entry to correct, then key the correction(s) to the journal entry and click on the **Post** button (or press Enter).

7. Display the income statement, balance sheet, and statement of owner's equity.

   Click on the **Reports** toolbar button and click on **Financial Statements.** Click on **Income Statement, Balance Sheet,** and **Statement of Owner's Equity.** To print each report, click on the **Print** button.

8. Click on the **Save** toolbar button to save your data file.

Problem 3–5A
Adjusting entries and adjusted trial balances
Objectives 3, 4

Atwater Service Co., which specializes in appliance repair services, is owned and operated by Carri Atwater. Atwater Service Co.'s accounting clerk prepared the following trial balance at December 31, the end of the current year:

Atwater Service Co.
Trial Balance
December 31, 20—

Cash..	3,200	
Accounts Receivable...	17,200	
Prepaid Insurance	3,900	
Supplies	2,450	
Land	50,000	
Building	141,500	
Accumulated Depreciation—Building		95,700
Equipment...	90,100	
Accumulated Depreciation—Equipment.............		65,300
Accounts Payable		7,500
Unearned Rent...		4,000
Carri Atwater, Capital.......................................		65,900
Carri Atwater, Drawing	5,000	
Fees Earned..		218,400
Salaries and Wages Expense	78,700	
Utilities Expense..	28,200	
Advertising Expense	19,000	
Repairs Expense..	13,500	
Miscellaneous Expense	4,050	
	456,800	456,800

The data needed to determine year-end adjustments are as follows:

  a. Depreciation of building for the year, $1,500.
  b. Depreciation of equipment for the year, $5,500.
  c. Accrued salaries and wages at December 31, $1,150.
  d. Unexpired insurance at December 31, $1,100.
  e. Fees earned but unbilled on December 31, $4,950.
  f. Supplies on hand at December 31, $500.
  g. Rent unearned at December 31, $1,500.

Instructions

1. Journalize the adjusting entries. Add additional accounts as needed.

2. Determine the balances of the accounts affected by the adjusting entries and prepare an adjusted trial balance.

DOS Instructions

1. Load the General Ledger Software program (IA1) from the program disk.

   Key **IA1** and press Enter at the DOS prompt. To the question "Read About General Ledger Software?" select **No** to bypass the copyright screens.

2. Load the file **03-5A** from the program disk.

   Press the **Alt** key to activate menu selection. Choose the **Open Accounting File** command in the File menu. Select the **Files** button and choose the accounting file to open. Select the Ok button to open the file.

3. Carefully key your name in the Student Name field in the General Information window. Press Ctrl+Enter to select Ok.

4. Choose the **Save As** command in the File menu and save the file to the drive and directory containing your data files. Key a file name of XXX3-5A (where XXX are your initials). Press Ctrl+Enter to select Ok.

5. Key the adjusting entries in the General Journal.

   Type the current year and enter 12/31 as the date for each entry. Key the letter for each adjusting entry in the Reference field; for example, (a), (b), etc. To display a list of accounts, press the F1 key. After each entry is keyed, press Ctrl+Enter to select Ok. When the Posting Summary window appears, press Ctrl+Enter to Post.

6. Display the adjusting entries.

   Select **Journals** from the Reports menu and select **General Journal** in the Report Selection window. Select the Ok button in the Selection Options window to display the adjusting entries. Press the F9 key to print the general journal report.

7. Make corrections to the adjusting entries, if necessary.

   Select **List** in the General Journal window to display the adjusting entries. Select the entry for correction and make the necessary change(s).

8. Display the income statement, balance sheet, and statement of owner's equity.

   Select **Financial Statements** from the Reports menu and select **Income Statement, Balance Sheet,** and **Statement of Owner's Equity** in the Report Selection window. Press the F9 key to print each report.

9. Choose the **Save Accounting File** command in the File menu to save your data file.

Windows Instructions

To access Help, click on the Help button that appears in most windows.

1. Click on the **Open** toolbar button and double-click on 03-5A to open the file.

2. Carefully key your name in the User Name field and click on the OK button.

3. Click on the **Save As** toolbar button and save the file to the drive and directory containing your data files. Key a file name of XXX3-5A (where XXX are your initials). Click on the OK button.

4. Click on the **Journal** toolbar button and key the adjusting entries in the General Journal.

   Key 12/31/-- (where -- is the current year) as the date for each entry. Key the letter for each adjusting entry in the Reference field; for example, (a), (b), etc. After each entry is keyed, click on the **Post** button (or press Enter).

5. Display the adjusting entries.

   Click on the **Reports** toolbar button and click on **Journals** in the Report Selection window. Click on **General Journal** and the OK button to choose a report to display. Click on **Include All Journal Entries** and the OK button to display the adjusting entries report. To print the report, click on the **Print** button.

6. Make corrections to the adjusting entries, if necessary.

In the General Journal window, click on the entry to correct, then key the correction(s) to the journal entry and click on the **Post** button (or press Enter).

7. Display the income statement, balance sheet, and statement of owner's equity.

Click on the **Reports** toolbar button and click on **Financial Statements**.   Click on **Income Statement, Balance Sheet,** and **Statement of Owner's Equity.** To print each report, click on the **Print** button.

8. Click on the **Save** toolbar button to save your data file.

Problem 3–4B
Adjusting entries
Objective 3

Icarus Company, an electronics repair store, prepared the following trial balance at the end of its first year of operations:

Icarus Company
Trial Balance
June 30, 20—

Cash	1,150	
Accounts Receivable	5,500	
Supplies	1,800	
Equipment	17,900	
Accounts Payable		750
Unearned Fees		2,000
Sonja Ash, Capital		10,000
Sonja Ash, Drawing	1,500	
Fees Earned		35,250
Wages Expense	8,500	
Rent Expense	8,000	
Utilities Expense	2,750	
Miscellaneous Expense	900	
	48,000	48,000

For preparing the adjusting entries, the following data were assembled:

a. Fees earned but unbilled on June 30 were $1,200.
b. Supplies on hand on June 30 were $290.
c. Depreciation of equipment was estimated to be $1,000 for the year.
d. The balance in unearned fees represented the April 1 receipt in advance for services to be provided. Only $700 of the services was provided between April 1 and June 30.
e. Unpaid wages accrued on June 30 were $140.

Instructions

Journalize the adjusting entries necessary on June 30.

DOS Instructions

1. Load the General Ledger Software program (IA1) from the program disk.

Key **IA1** and press Enter at the DOS prompt. To the question "Read About General Ledger Software?" select **No** to bypass the copyright screens.

2. Load the file **03-4B** from the program disk.

Press the **Alt** key to activate menu selection. Choose the **Open Accounting File** command in the File menu. Select the **Files** button and choose the accounting file to open. Select the Ok button to open the file.

3. Carefully key your name in the Student Name field in the General Information window. Press Ctrl+Enter to select Ok.

4. Choose the **Save As** command in the File menu and save the file to the drive and directory containing your data files. Key a file name of XXX3-4B (where XXX are your initials). Press Ctrl+Enter to select Ok.

5. Key the adjusting entries in the General Journal.

Type the current year and enter 06/31 as the date for each entry. Key the letter for each adjusting entry in the Reference field; for example, (a), (b), etc. To display a list of accounts, press the F1 key. After each journal entry is keyed, press Ctrl+Enter to select Ok. When the Posting Summary window appears, press Ctrl+Enter to Post.

6. Display the adjusting entries.

   Select **Journals** from the Reports menu and select **General Journal** in the Report Selection window. Select the Ok button in the Selection Options window to display the adjusting entries. Press the F9 key to print the general journal report.

7. Make corrections to the adjusting entries, if necessary.

   Select **List** in the General Journal window to display the adjusting entries. Select the entry for correction and make the necessary change(s).

8. Display the income statement, balance sheet, and statement of owner's equity.

   Select **Financial Statements** from the Reports menu and select **Income Statement, Balance Sheet,** and **Statement of Owner's Equity** in the Report Selection window. Press the F9 key to print each report.

9. Choose the **Save Accounting File** command in the File menu to save your data file.

Windows Instructions

To access Help, click on the Help button that appears in most windows.

1. Click on the **Open** toolbar button and double-click on 03-4B to open the file.

2. Carefully key your name in the User Name field and click on the OK button.

3. Click on the **Save As** toolbar button and save the file to the drive and directory containing your data files. Key a file name of XXX3-4B (where XXX are your initials). Click on the OK button.

4. Click on the **Journal** toolbar button and key the adjusting entries in the General Journal.

   Key 06/30/-- (where -- is the current year) as the date for each entry. Key the letter for each adjusting entry in the Reference field; for example, (a), (b), etc. After each entry is keyed, click on the **Post** button (or press Enter).

5. Display the adjusting entries.

   Click on the **Reports** toolbar button and click on **Journals** in the Report Selection window. Click on **General Journal** and the OK button to choose a report to display. Click on **Include All Journal Entries** and the OK button to display the adjusting entries report. To print the report, click on the **Print** button.

6. Make corrections to the adjusting entries, if necessary.

   In the General Journal window, click on the entry to correct, then key the correction(s) to the journal entry and click on the **Post** button (or press Enter).

7. Display the income statement, balance sheet, and statement of owner's equity.

   Click on the **Reports** toolbar button and click on **Financial Statements**. Click on **Income Statement, Balance Sheet,** and **Statement of Owner's Equity.** To print each report, click on the **Print** button.

8. Click on the **Save** toolbar button to save your data file.

Problem 3–5B
Adjusting entries and
adjusted trial balance
Objectives 3, 4

Zornes Company is a small editorial services company owned and operated by Valerie Spann. Zornes Company's accounting clerk prepared the following trial balance on December 31, the end of the current year:

Zornes Company
Trial Balance
December 31, 20—

Cash..	6,700	
Accounts Receivable...	23,800	
Prepaid Insurance...	3,400	
Supplies	1,950	
Land...	50,000	
Building	141,500	
Accumulated Depreciation—Building		91,700
Equipment...	90,100	
Accumulated Depreciation—Equipment.............		65,300
Accounts Payable		7,500
Unearned Rent..		6,000
Valerie Spann, Capital		81,500
Valerie Spann, Drawing	10,000	
Fees Earned..		218,400
Salaries and Wages Expense	80,200	
Utilities Expense...	28,200	
Advertising Expense	19,000	
Repairs Expense...	11,500	
Miscellaneous Expense	4,050	
	470,400	470,400

The data needed to determine year-end adjustments are as follows:

a. Unexpired insurance at December 31, $1,200.
b. Supplies on hand at December 31, $500.
c. Depreciation of building for the year, $1,620.
d. Depreciation of equipment for the year, $5,500.
e. Rent unearned at December 31, $2,000.
f. Accrued salaries and wages at December 31, $1,300.
g. Fees earned but unbilled on December 31, $3,750.

Instructions

1. Journalize the adjusting entries. Add additional accounts as needed.
2. Determine the balances of the accounts affected by the adjusting entries and prepare an adjusted trial balance.

DOS Instructions

1. Load the General Ledger Software program (IA1) from the program disk.

   Key **IA1** and press Enter at the DOS prompt. To the question "Read About General Ledger Software?" select **No** to bypass the copyright screens.

2. Load the file **03-5B** from the program disk.

   Press the **Alt** key to activate menu selection. Choose the **Open Accounting File** command in the File menu. Select the **Files** button and choose the accounting file to open. Select the Ok button to open the file.

3. Carefully key your name in the Student Name field in the General Information window. Press Ctrl+Enter to select Ok.

4. Choose the **Save As** command in the File menu and save the file to the drive and directory containing your data files. Key a file name of XXX3-5B (where XXX are your initials). Press Ctrl+Enter to select Ok.

5. Key the adjusting entries in the General Journal.

   Type the current year and enter 12/31 as the date for each entry. Key the letter for each adjusting entry in the Reference field; for example, (a), (b), etc. To display a list of accounts, press the F1 key. After each entry is keyed, press Ctrl+Enter to select Ok. When the Posting Summary window appears, press Ctrl+Enter to Post.

6. Display the adjusting entries.

   Select **Journals** from the Reports menu and select **General Journal** in the Report Selection window. Select the Ok button in the Selection Options window to display the adjusting entries. Press the F9 key to print the general journal report.

7. Make corrections to the adjusting entries, if necessary.

   Select **List** in the General Journal window to display the adjusting entries. Select the entry for correction and make the necessary change(s).

8. Display the income statement, balance sheet, and statement of owner's equity.

   Select **Financial Statements** from the Reports menu and select **Income Statement, Balance Sheet,** and **Statement of Owner's Equity** in the Report Selection window. Press the F9 key to print each report.

9. Choose the **Save Accounting File** command in the File menu to save your data file.

Windows Instructions   **To access Help, click on the Help button that appears in most windows.**

1. Click on the **Open** toolbar button and double-click on 03-5B to open the file.

2. Carefully key your name in the User Name field and click on the OK button.

3. Click on the **Save As** toolbar button and save the file to the drive and directory containing your data files. Key a file name of XXX3-5B (where XXX are your initials). Click on the OK button.

4. Click on the **Journal** toolbar button and key the adjusting entries in the General Journal.

   Key 12/31/-- (where -- is the current year) as the date for each entry. Key the letter for each adjusting entry in the Reference field; for example, (a), (b), etc. After each entry is keyed, click on the **Post** button (or press Enter).

5. Display the adjusting entries.

   Click on the **Reports** toolbar button and click on **Journals** in the Report Selection window. Click on **General Journal** and the OK button to choose a report to display. Click on **Include All Journal Entries** and the OK button to display the adjusting entries report. To print the report, click on the **Print** button.

6. Make corrections to the adjusting entries, if necessary.

   In the General Journal window, click on the entry to correct, then key the correction(s) to the journal entry and click on the **Post** button (or press Enter).

7. Display the income statement, balance sheet, and statement of owner's equity.

   Click on the **Reports** toolbar button and click on **Financial Statements**. Click on **Income Statement, Balance Sheet,** and **Statement of Owner's Equity**. To print each report, click on the **Print** button.

8. Click on the **Save** toolbar button to save your data file.

Problem 4–1A
Work sheet and related items
Objectives 1, 2, 3

The trial balance of Wonder Wash Laundry at August 31, 2000, the end of the current fiscal year, and the data needed to determine year-end adjustments are as follows:

Wonder Wash Laundry
Trial Balance
August 31, 2000

Cash...	13,100	
Laundry Supplies	6,560	
Prepaid Insurance	4,490	
Laundry Equipment..	95,100	
Accumulated Depreciation		40,200
Accounts Payable		6,100
Louis Krupman, Capital...		37,800
Louis Krupman, Drawing...	2,000	
Laundry Revenue...		140,900
Wages Expense...	51,400	
Rent Expense...	36,000	
Utilities Expense..	13,650	
Miscellaneous Expense	2,700	
	225,000	225,000

a. Wages accrued but not paid at August 31 are $1,350.
b. Depreciation of equipment during the year is $6,600.
c. Laundry supplies on hand at August 31 are $1,500.
d. Insurance premiums expired during the year are $2,800.

Instructions

1. Enter the trial balance on a ten-column work sheet and complete the work sheet. Add accounts as needed.
2. Prepare an income statement, a statement of owner's equity (no additional investments were made during the year), and a balance sheet.
3. On the basis of the adjustment data in the work sheet, journalize the adjusting entries.
4. On the basis of the data in the work sheet, journalize the closing entries.

DOS Instructions

1. Load the General Ledger Software program (IA1) from the program disk.

   Key **IA1** and press Enter at the DOS prompt. To the question "Read About General Ledger Software?" select **No** to bypass the copyright screens.

2. Load the file **04-1A** from the program disk.

   Press the **Alt** key to activate menu selection. Choose the **Open Accounting File** command in the File menu. Select the **Files** button and choose the accounting file to open. Select the Ok button to open the file.

3. Carefully key your name in the Student Name field in the General Information window. Press Ctrl+Enter to select Ok.

4. Choose the **Save As** command in the File menu and save the file to the drive and directory containing your data files. Key a file name of XXX4-1A (where XXX are your initials). Press Ctrl+Enter to select Ok.

5. Key the adjusting entries in the General Journal.

   Key 2000 as the current year and enter 08/31 as the date for each entry. Key the letter for each adjusting entry in the Reference field; for example, (a), (b), etc. To display a list of accounts, press the F1 key. After each entry is keyed, press Ctrl+Enter to select Ok. When the Posting Summary window appears, press Ctrl+Enter to Post.

6. Display the adjusting entries.

   Select **Journals** from the Reports menu and select **General Journal** in the Report Selection window. Select the Ok button in the Selection Options window to display the adjusting entries. Press the F9 key to print the general journal report.

7. Make corrections to the adjusting entries, if necessary.

Select **List** in the General Journal window to display the adjusting entries. Select the entry for correction and make the necessary change(s).

8. Display the income statement, balance sheet, and statement of owner's equity.

    Select **Financial Statements** from the Reports menu and select **Income Statement, Balance Sheet,** and **Statement of Owner's Equity** in the Report Selection window. Press the F9 key to print the financial statements.

9. Choose the **Save Accounting File** command in the File menu.

10. Perform period-end closing.

    Choose **Period-End Closing** from the Options menu. When the dialog box appears, press Ctrl+Enter to select Ok.

11. Display a post-closing trial balance.

    Select **Ledgers** from the Reports menu and select **Trial Balance** in the Report Selection window. Press the F9 key to print the trial balance report.

12. Choose the **Save As** command in the File menu to save your data file. Key a file name of XXX4-1AP (where XXX are your initials, 4-1A represents the problem number, and P represents post closing). Press Ctrl+Enter to select Ok.

Windows Instructions   **To access Help, click on the Help button that appears in most windows.**

1. Click on the **Open** toolbar button and double-click on 04-1A to open the file.

2. Carefully key your name in the User Name field and click on the OK button.

3. Click on the **Save As** toolbar button and save the file to the drive and directory containing your data files. Key a file name of XXX4-1A (where XXX are your initials). Click on the OK button.

4. Click on the **Journal** toolbar button and key the adjusting entries in the General Journal.

    Key 08/31/00 as the date for each entry. Key the letter for each adjusting entry in the Reference field: for example, (a), (b), etc. After each entry is keyed, click on the **Post** button (or press Enter).

5. Display the adjusting entries.

    Click on the **Reports** toolbar button and click on **Journals** in the Report Selection window. Click on **General Journal** and the OK button to choose a report to display. Click on **Include All Journal Entries** and the OK button to display the adjusting entries. To print the report, click on the **Print** button.

6. Make corrections to the adjusting entries, if necessary.

    In the General Journal window, click on the entry to correct, then key the correction(s) to the journal entry and click on the **Post** button (or press Enter).

7. Display the income statement, balance sheet, and statement of owner's equity.

    Click on the **Reports** toolbar button and click on **Financial Statements**. Click on **Income Statement, Balance Sheet,** and **Statement of Owner's Equity**. To print each report, click on the **Print** button.

8. Click on the **Save** toolbar button to save your file.

9. Click on **Generate Closing Journal Entries** in the Options menu. When the dialog box appears, click on the **Yes** button. When the closing entries appear, click on the **Post** button.

10. Display a post-closing trial balance.

    Click on the **Reports** toolbar button and click on **Ledger Reports**. Click on **Trial Balance** and the OK button to choose a report to display. To print the report, click on the **Print** button.

11. Click on the **Save As** toolbar button to save your data file. Key a file name of XXX4-1AP (where XXX are your initials, 4-1A represents the problem number, and P represents post closing). Click on the OK button.

Problem 4–4A
Work sheet and financial statements
Objectives 1, 2

Last Chance Company offers legal consulting advice to death-row inmates. Last Chance Company prepared the following trial balance at April 30, 2000, the end of the current fiscal year:

Last Chance Company
Trial Balance
April 30, 2000

Cash..	3,200	
Accounts Receivable...	10,500	
Prepaid Insurance...	3,800	
Supplies	1,950	
Land..	50,000	
Building	137,500	
Accumulated Depreciation—Building.................		51,700
Equipment..	90,100	
Accumulated Depreciation—Equipment.............		35,300
Accounts Payable		7,500
Unearned Rent..		3,000
Jason Soroka, Capital		164,100
Jason Soroka, Drawing	10,000	
Fees Revenue...		198,400
Salaries and Wages Expense	80,200	
Advertising Expense	38,200	
Utilities Expense...	19,000	
Repairs Expense...	11,500	
Miscellaneous Expense	4,050	
	460,000	460,000

The data needed to determine year-end adjustments are as follows:
 a. Accrued fees revenue at April 30 is $3,800.
 b. Insurance expired during the year is $2,900.
 c. Supplies on hand at April 30 are $450.
 d. Depreciation of building for the year is $1,620.
 e. Depreciation of equipment for the year is $3,500.
 f. Accrued salaries and wages at April 30 are $2,050.
 g. Unearned rent at April 30 is $1,000.

Instructions

1. Enter the trial balance on a ten-column work sheet and complete the work sheet. Add accounts as needed.
2. Prepare an income statement for the year ended April 30.
3. Prepare a statement of owner's equity for the year ended April 30. No additional investments were made during the year.
4. Prepare a balance sheet as of April 30.
5. Compute the percent of net income to total revenue for the year.

DOS Instructions

1. Load the General Ledger Software program (IA1) from the program disk.

   Key **IA1** and press Enter at the DOS prompt. To the question "Read About General Ledger Software?" select **No** to bypass the copyright screens.

2. Load the file **04-4A** from the program disk.

   Press the **Alt** key to activate menu selection. Choose the **Open Accounting File** command in the File menu. Select the **Files** button and choose the accounting file to open. Select the Ok button to open the file.

3. Carefully key your name in the Student Name field in the General Information window. Press Ctrl+Enter to select Ok.

4. Choose the **Save As** command in the File menu and save the file to the drive and directory containing your data files. Key a file name of XXX4-4A (where XXX are your initials). Press Ctrl+Enter to select Ok.

5. Key the adjusting entries in the General Journal.

Key 2000 as the current year and enter 04/30 as the date for each entry. Key the letter for each adjusting entry in the Reference field; for example, (a), (b), etc. To display a list of accounts, press the F1 key. After each entry is keyed, press Ctrl+Enter to select Ok. When the Posting Summary window appears, press Ctrl+Enter to Post.

6. Display the adjusting entries.

   Select **Journals** from the Reports menu and select **General Journal** in the Report Selection window. Select the Ok button in the Selection Options window to display the adjusting entries. Press the F9 key to print the general journal report.

7. Make corrections to the adjusting entries, if necessary.

   Select **List** in the General Journal window to display the adjusting entries. Select the entry for correction and make the necessary change(s).

8. Display the income statement, balance sheet, and statement of owner's equity.

   Select **Financial Statements** from the Reports menu and select **Income Statement, Balance Sheet,** and **Statement of Owner's Equity** in the Report Selection window. Press the F9 key to print the financial statements.

9. Choose the **Save Accounting File** command in the File menu.

10. Perform period-end closing.

    Choose **Period-End Closing** from the Options menu. When the dialog box appears, press Ctrl+Enter to select Ok.

11. Display a post-closing trial balance.

    Select **Ledgers** from the Reports menu and select **Trial Balance** in the Report Selection window. Press the F9 key to print the trial balance report.

12. Choose the **Save As** command in the File menu to save your data file. Key a file name of XXX4-4AP (where XXX are your initials, 4-4A represents the problem number, and P represents post closing). Press Ctrl+Enter to select Ok.

Windows Instructions   **To access Help, click on the Help button that appears in most windows.**

1. Click on the **Open** toolbar button and double-click on 04-4A to open the file.

2. Carefully key your name in the User Name field and click on the OK button.

3. Click on the **Save As** toolbar button and save the file to the drive and directory containing your data files. Key a file name of XXX4-4A (where XXX are your initials). Click on the OK button.

4. Click on the **Journal** toolbar button and key the adjusting entries in the General Journal.

   Key 04/30/00 as the date for each entry. Key the letter for each adjusting entry in the Reference field: for example, (a), (b), etc. After each entry is keyed, click on the **Post** button (or press Enter).

5. Display the adjusting entries.

   Click on the **Reports** toolbar button and click on **Journals** in the Report Selection window. Click on **General Journal** and the OK button to choose a report to display. Click on **Include All Journal Entries** and the OK button to display the adjusting entries report. To print the report, click on the **Print** button.

6. Make corrections to the adjusting entries, if necessary.

   In the General Journal window, click on the entry to correct, then key the correction(s) to the journal entry and click on the **Post** button (or press Enter).

7. Display the income statement, balance sheet, and statement of owner's equity.

   Click on the **Reports** toolbar button and click on **Financial Statements**. Click on **Income Statement, Balance Sheet,** and **Statement of Owner's Equity.** To print each report, click on the **Print** button.

8. Click on the **Save** toolbar button to save your file.

9. Click on **Generate Closing Journal Entries** in the Options menu. When the dialog box appears, click on the **Yes** button. When the closing entries appear, click on the **Post** button.

10. Display a post-closing trial balance.

Click on the **Reports** toolbar button and click on **Ledger Reports**. Click on **Trial Balance** and the OK button to choose a report to display. To print the report, click on the **Print** button.

11. Click on the **Save As** toolbar button to save your data file. Key a file name of XXX4-4AP (where XXX are your initials, 4-4A represents the problem number, and P represents post closing). Click on the OK button.

Problem 4–5A
*Ledger accounts, work
sheet, and related items*
Objectives 1, 2, 3

The trial balance of Avery Repairs at December 31, 2000, the end of the current year, and the data needed to determine year-end adjustments are as follows:

Avery Repairs
Trial Balance
December 31, 2000

11	Cash	6,825	
13	Supplies	4,820	
14	Prepaid Insurance	3,500	
16	Equipment	42,200	
17	Accumulated Depreciation—Equipment		9,050
18	Trucks	45,000	
19	Accumulated Depreciation—Trucks		27,100
21	Accounts Payable		4,015
31	Steve Galvine, Capital		29,885
32	Steve Galvine, Drawing	3,000	
41	Service Revenue		99,950
51	Wages Expense	42,010	
53	Rent Expense	10,100	
55	Truck Expense	9,350	
59	Miscellaneous Expense	3,195	
		170,000	170,000

a. Supplies on hand at December 31 are $1,100.
b. Insurance premiums expired during year are $2,500.
c. Depreciation of equipment during year is $6,080.
d. Depreciation of trucks during year is $5,500.
e. Wages accrued but not paid at December 31 are $600.

Instructions

1. For each account listed in the trial balance, enter the balance in the appropriate Balance column of a four-column account and place a check mark (✓) in the Posting Reference column.
2. Enter the trial balance on a ten-column work sheet and complete the work sheet. Add accounts as needed.
3. Prepare an income statement, a statement of owner's equity (no additional investments were made during the year), and a balance sheet.
4. Journalize and post the adjusting entries, inserting balances in the accounts affected. The following additional accounts from Avery's chart of accounts should be used: Wages Payable, 22; Supplies Expense, 52; Depreciation Expense—Equipment, 54; Depreciation Expense—Trucks, 56; Insurance Expense, 57.
5. Journalize and post the closing entries. (Income Summary is account #33 in the chart of accounts.) Indicate closed accounts by inserting a line in both Balance columns opposite the closing entry.
6. Prepare a post-closing trial balance.

DOS Instructions

1. Load the General Ledger Software program (IA1) from the program disk.

Key **IA1** and press Enter at the DOS prompt. To the question "Read About General Ledger Software?" select **No** to bypass the copyright screens.

2. Load the file **04-5A** from the program disk.

Press the **Alt** key to activate menu selection. Choose the **Open Accounting File** command in the File menu. Select the **Files** button and choose the accounting file to open. Select the Ok button to open the file.

3. Carefully key your name in the Student Name field in the General Information window. Press Ctrl+Enter to select Ok.

4. Choose the **Save As** command in the File menu and save the file to the drive and directory containing your data files. Key a file name of XXX4-5A (where XXX are your initials). Press Ctrl+Enter to select Ok.

5. Key the adjusting entries in the General Journal.

   Key 2000 as the current year and enter 12/31 as the date for each entry. Key the letter for each adjusting entry in the Reference field; for example, (a), (b), etc. To display a list of accounts, press the F1 key. After each entry is keyed, press Ctrl+Enter to select Ok. When the Posting Summary window appears, press Ctrl+Enter to Post.

6. Display the adjusting entries.

   Select **Journals** from the Reports menu and select **General Journal** in the Report Selection window. Select the Ok button in the Selection Options window to display the adjusting entries. Press the F9 key to print the general journal report.

7. Make corrections to the adjusting entries, if necessary.

   Select **List** in the General Journal window to display the adjusting entries. Select the entry for correction and make the necessary change(s).

8. Display the income statement, balance sheet, and statement of owner's equity.

   Select **Financial Statements** from the Reports menu and select **Income Statement, Balance Sheet,** and **Statement of Owner's Equity** in the Report Selection window. Press the F9 key to print the financial statements.

9. Choose the **Save Accounting File** command in the File menu.

10. Perform period-end closing.

    Choose **Period-End Closing** from the Options menu. When the dialog box appears, press Ctrl+Enter to select Ok.

11. Display a post-closing trial balance.

    Select **Ledgers** from the Reports menu and select **Trial Balance** in the Report Selection window. Press the F9 key to print the trial balance report.

12. Choose the **Save As** command in the File menu to save your data file. Key a file name of XXX4-5AP (where XXX are your initials, 4-5A represents the problem number, and P represents post closing). Press Ctrl+Enter to select Ok.

Windows Instructions   **To access Help, click on the Help button that appears in most windows.**

1. Click on the **Open** toolbar button and double-click on 04-5A to open the file.

2. Carefully key your name in the User Name field and click on the OK button.

3. Click on the **Save As** toolbar button and save the file to the drive and directory containing your data files. Key a file name of XXX4-5A (where XXX are your initials). Click on the OK button.

4. Click on the **Journal** toolbar button and key the adjusting entries in the General Journal.

   Key 12/31/00 as the date for each entry. Key the letter for each adjusting entry in the Reference field: for example, (a), (b), etc. After each entry is keyed, click on the **Post** button (or press Enter).

5. Display the adjusting entries.

   Click on the **Reports** toolbar button and click on **Journals** in the Report Selection window. Click on **General Journal** and the OK button to choose a report to display. Click on **Include All**

Journal Entries and the OK button to display the adjusting entries report. To print the report, click on the **Print** button.

6. Make corrections to the adjusting entries, if necessary.

   In the General Journal window, click on the entry to correct, then key the correction(s) to the journal entry and click on the **Post** button (or press Enter).

7. Display the income statement, balance sheet, and statement of owner's equity.

   Click on the **Reports** toolbar button and click on **Financial Statements**. Click on **Income Statement, Balance Sheet,** and **Statement of Owner's Equity**. To print each report, click on the **Print** button.

8. Click on the **Save** toolbar button to save your file.

9. Click on **Generate Closing Journal Entries** in the Options menu. When the dialog box appears, click on the **Yes** button. When the closing entries appear, click on the **Post** button.

10. Display a post-closing trial balance.

    Click on the **Reports** toolbar button and click on **Ledger Reports**. Click on **Trial Balance** and the OK button to choose a report to display. To print the report, click on the **Print** button.

11. Click on the **Save As** toolbar button to save your data file. Key a file name of XXX4-5AP (where XXX are your initials, 4-5A represents the problem number, and P represents post closing). Click on the OK button.

Problem 4–1B
Work sheet and related items
Objectives 1, 2, 3

The trial balance of The Wash and Dry Laundromat at July 31, 2000, the end of the current fiscal year, and the data needed to determine year-end adjustments are as follows:

The Wash and Dry Laundromat
Trial Balance
July 31, 2000

Cash	6,290	
Laundry Supplies	5,850	
Prepaid Insurance	2,400	
Laundry Equipment	99,750	
Accumulated Depreciation		52,700
Accounts Payable		6,950
Nikki Weiss, Capital		37,450
Nikki Weiss, Drawing	4,000	
Laundry Revenue		67,900
Wages Expense	22,900	
Rent Expense	14,400	
Utilities Expense	8,500	
Miscellaneous Expense	910	
	165,000	165,000

a. Laundry supplies on hand at March 31 are $1,240.
b. Insurance premiums expired during the year are $1,700.
c. Depreciation of equipment during the year is $6,200.
d. Wages accrued but not paid at March 31 are $1,050.

Instructions

1. Enter the trial balance on a ten-column work sheet and complete the work sheet. Add accounts as needed.
2. Prepare an income statement, a statement of owner's equity (no additional investments were made during the year), and a balance sheet.
3. On the basis of the adjustment data in the work sheet, journalize the adjusting entries.
4. On the basis of the data in the work sheet, journalize the closing entries.

DOS Instructions

1. Load the General Ledger Software program (IA1) from the program disk.

    Key **IA1** and press Enter at the DOS prompt. To the question "Read About General Ledger Software?" select **No** to bypass the copyright screens.

2. Load the file **04-1B** from the program disk.

    Press the **Alt** key to activate menu selection. Choose the **Open Accounting File** command in the File menu. Select the **Files** button and choose the accounting file to open. Select the Ok button to open the file.

3. Carefully key your name in the Student Name field in the General Information window. Press Ctrl+Enter to select Ok.

4. Choose the **Save As** command in the File menu and save the file to the drive and directory containing your data files. Key a file name of XXX4-1B (where XXX are your initials). Press Ctrl+Enter to select Ok.

5. Key the adjusting entries in the General Journal.

    Key 2000 as the current year and enter 07/31 as the date for each entry. Key the letter for each adjusting entry in the Reference field; for example, (a), (b), etc. To display a list of accounts, press the F1 key. After each entry is keyed, press Ctrl+Enter to select Ok. When the Posting Summary window appears, press Ctrl+Enter to Post.

6. Display the adjusting entries.

    Select **Journals** from the Reports menu and select **General Journal** in the Report Selection window. Select the Ok button in the Selection Options window to display the adjusting entries. Press the F9 key to print the general journal report.

7. Make corrections to the adjusting entries, if necessary.

    Select **List** in the General Journal window to display the adjusting entries. Select the entry for correction and make the necessary change(s).

8. Display the income statement, balance sheet, and statement of owner's equity.

    Select **Financial Statements** from the Reports menu and select **Income Statement, Balance Sheet,** and **Statement of Owner's Equity** in the Report Selection window. Press the F9 key to print the financial statements.

9. Choose the **Save Accounting File** command in the File menu.

10. Perform period-end closing.

    Choose **Period-End Closing** from the Options menu. When the dialog box appears, press Ctrl+Enter to select Ok.

11. Display a post-closing trial balance.

    Select **Ledgers** from the Reports menu and select **Trial Balance** in the Report Selection window. Press the F9 key to print the trial balance report.

12. Choose the **Save As** command in the File menu to save your data file. Key a file name of XXX4-1BP (where XXX are your initials, 4-1B represents the problem number, and P represents post closing). Press Ctrl+Enter to select Ok.

Windows Instructions

To access Help, click on the Help button that appears in most windows.

1. Click on the **Open** toolbar button and double-click on 04-1B to open the file.

2. Carefully key your name in the User Name field and click on the OK button.

3. Click on the **Save As** toolbar button and save the file to the drive and directory containing your data files. Key a file name of XXX4-1B (where XXX are your initials). Click on the OK button.

4. Click on the **Journal** toolbar button and key the adjusting entries in the General Journal.

Key 07/31/00 as the date for each entry. Key the letter for each adjusting entry in the Reference field: for example, (a), (b), etc. After each entry is keyed, click on the **Post** button (or press Enter).

5. Display the adjusting entries.

   Click on the **Reports** toolbar button and click on **Journals** in the Report Selection window. Click on **General Journal** and the OK button to choose a report to display. Click on **Include All Journal Entries** and the OK button to display the adjusting entries report. To print the report, click on the **Print** button.

6. Make corrections to the adjusting entries, if necessary.

   In the General Journal window, click on the entry to correct, then key the correction(s) to the journal entry and click on the **Post** button (or press Enter).

7. Display the income statement, balance sheet, and statement of owner's equity.

   Click on the **Reports** toolbar button and click on **Financial Statements**. Click on **Income Statement, Balance Sheet,** and **Statement of Owner's Equity**. To print each report, click on the **Print** button.

8. Click on the **Save** toolbar button to save your file.

9. Click on **Generate Closing Journal Entries** in the Options menu. When the dialog box appears, click on the **Yes** button. When the closing entries appear, click on the **Post** button.

10. Display a post-closing trial balance.

    Click on the **Reports** toolbar button and click on **Ledger Reports**. Click on **Trial Balance** and the OK button to choose a report to display. To print the report, click on the **Print** button.

11. Click on the **Save As** toolbar button to save your data file. Key a file name of XXX4-1BP (where XXX are your initials, 4-1B represents the problem number, and P represents post closing). Click on the OK button.

Problem 4–4B
Work sheet and financial statements
Objectives 1, 2

Koontz Company maintains and repairs warning lights, such as those found on radio towers and light-houses. Koontz Company prepared the following trial balance at May 31, 2000, the end of the current fiscal year:

Koontz Company
Trial Balance
May 31, 2000

Cash	7,500	
Accounts Receivable	16,500	
Prepaid Insurance	2,600	
Supplies	1,950	
Land	60,000	
Building	100,500	
Accumulated Depreciation—Building		81,700
Equipment	72,400	
Accumulated Depreciation—Equipment		63,800
Accounts Payable		6,100
Unearned Rent		1,500
Joe Carpenter, Capital		60,700
Joe Carpenter, Drawing	4,000	
Fees Revenue		161,200
Salaries and Wages Expense	60,200	
Advertising Expense	19,000	
Utilities Expense	18,200	
Repairs Expense	8,100	
Miscellaneous Expense	4,050	
	375,000	375,000

The data needed to determine year-end adjustments are as follows:

    a. Fees revenue accrued at May 31 is $3,500.
    b. Insurance expired during the year is $1,000.
    c. Supplies on hand at May 31 are $450.
    d. Depreciation of building for the year is $1,620.
    e. Depreciation of equipment for the year is $3,160.
    f. Accrued salaries and wages at May 31 are $1,700.
    g. Unearned rent at May 31 is $1,000.

Instructions

1. Enter the trial balance on a ten-column work sheet and complete the work sheet. Add accounts as needed.
2. Prepare an income statement for the year ended May 31.
3. Prepare a statement of owner's equity for the year ended May 31. No additional investments were made during the year.
4. Prepare a balance sheet as of May 31.
5. Compute the percent of net income to total revenue for the year.

DOS Instructions

1. Load the General Ledger Software program (IA1) from the program disk.

    Key **IA1** and press Enter at the DOS prompt. To the question "Read About General Ledger Software?" select **No** to bypass the copyright screens.

2. Load the file **04-4B** from the program disk.

    Press the **Alt** key to activate menu selection. Choose the **Open Accounting File** command in the File menu. Select the **Files** button and choose the accounting file to open. Select the Ok button to open the file.

3. Carefully key your name in the Student Name field in the General Information window. Press Ctrl+Enter to select Ok.

4. Choose the **Save As** command in the File menu and save the file to the drive and directory containing your data files. Key a file name of XXX4-4B (where XXX are your initials). Press Ctrl+Enter to select Ok.

5. Key the adjusting entries in the General Journal.

    Key 2000 as the current year and enter 05/31 as the date for each entry. Key the letter for each adjusting entry in the Reference field; for example, (a), (b), etc. To display a list of accounts, press the F1 key. After each entry is keyed, press Ctrl+Enter to select Ok. When the Posting Summary window appears, press Ctrl+Enter to Post.

6. Display the adjusting entries.

    Select **Journals** from the Reports menu and select **General Journal** in the Report Selection window. Select the Ok button in the Selection Options window to display the adjusting entries. Press the F9 key to print the general journal report.

7. Make corrections to the adjusting entries, if necessary.

    Select **List** in the General Journal window to display the adjusting entries. Select the entry for correction and make the necessary change(s).

8. Display the income statement, balance sheet, and statement of owner's equity.

    Select **Financial Statements** from the Reports menu and select **Income Statement, Balance Sheet,** and **Statement of Owner's Equity** in the Report Selection window. Press the F9 key to print the financial statements.

9. Choose the **Save Accounting File** command in the File menu.

10. Perform period-end closing.

    Choose **Period-End Closing** from the Options menu. When the dialog box appears, press Ctrl+Enter to select Ok.

11. Display a post-closing trial balance.

Select **Ledgers** from the Reports menu and select **Trial Balance** in the Report Selection window. Press the F9 key to print the trial balance report.

12. Choose the **Save As** command in the File menu to save your data file. Key a file name of XXX4-4BP (where XXX are your initials, 4-4B represents the problem number, and P represents post closing). Press Ctrl+Enter to select Ok.

Windows Instructions

To access Help, click on the Help button that appears in most windows.

1. Click on the **Open** toolbar button and double-click on 04-4B to open the file.

2. Carefully key your name in the User Name field and click on the OK button.

3. Click on the **Save As** toolbar button and save the file to the drive and directory containing your data files. Key a file name of XXX4-4B (where XXX are your initials). Click on the OK button.

4. Click on the **Journal** toolbar button and key the adjusting entries in the General Journal.

   Key 05/31/00 as the date for each entry. Key the letter for each adjusting entry in the Reference field: for example, (a), (b), etc. After each entry is keyed, click on the **Post** button (or press Enter).

5. Display the adjusting entries.

   Click on the **Reports** toolbar button and click on **Journals** in the Report Selection window. Click on **General Journal** and the OK button to choose a report to display. Click on **Include All Journal Entries** and the OK button to display the adjusting entries report. To print the report, click on the **Print** button.

6. Make corrections to the adjusting entries, if necessary.

   In the General Journal window, click on the entry to correct, then key the correction(s) to the journal entry and click on the **Post** button (or press Enter).

7. Display the income statement, balance sheet, and statement of owner's equity.

   Click on the **Reports** toolbar button and click on **Financial Statements**. Click on **Income Statement, Balance Sheet,** and **Statement of Owner's Equity.** To print each report, click on the **Print** button.

8. Click on the **Save** toolbar button to save your file.

9. Click on **Generate Closing Journal Entries** in the Options menu. When the dialog box appears, click on the **Yes** button. When the closing entries appear, click on the **Post** button.

10. Display a post-closing trial balance.

    Click on the **Reports** toolbar button and click on **Ledger Reports**. Click on **Trial Balance** and the OK button to choose a report to display. To print the report, click on the **Print** button.

11. Click on the **Save As** toolbar button to save your data file. Key a file name of XXX4-4BP (where XXX are your initials, 4-4B represents the problem number, and P represents post closing). Click on the OK button.

Problem 4–5B
Ledger accounts, work sheet, and related items
Objectives 1, 2, 3

The trial balance of Quick Repairs at March 31, 2000, the end of the current year, is shown at the top of the next page. The data needed to determine year-end adjustments are as follows:

a. Supplies on hand at March 31 are $1,205.
b. Insurance premiums expired during year are $935.
c. Depreciation of equipment during year is $3,380.
d. Depreciation of trucks during year is $4,400.
e. Wages accrued but not paid at March 31 are $800.

Quick Repairs
Trial Balance
March 31, 2000

11	Cash	6,950	
13	Supplies	4,295	
14	Prepaid Insurance	2,735	
16	Equipment	40,650	
17	Accumulated Depreciation—Equipment		11,209
18	Trucks	36,300	
19	Accumulated Depreciation—Trucks		6,400
21	Accounts Payable		2,015
31	Renee Dills, Capital		40,426
32	Renee Dills, Drawing	5,000	
41	Service Revenue		89,950
51	Wages Expense	33,925	
53	Rent Expense	9,600	
55	Truck Expense	8,350	
59	Miscellaneous Expense	2,195	
		150,000	150,000

Instructions

1. For each account listed in the trial balance, enter the balance in the appropriate Balance column of a four-column account and place a check mark (✓) in the Posting Reference column.
2. Enter the trial balance on a ten-column work sheet and complete the work sheet. Add accounts as needed.
3. Prepare an income statement, a statement of owner's equity (no additional investments were made during the year), and a balance sheet.
4. Journalize and post the adjusting entries, inserting balances in the accounts affected. The following additional accounts from Quick's chart of accounts should be used: Wages Payable, 22; Supplies Expense, 52; Depreciation Expense—Equipment, 54; Depreciation Expense—Trucks, 56; Insurance Expense, 57.
5. Journalize and post the closing entries. (Income Summary is account #33 in the chart of accounts.) Indicate closed accounts by inserting a line in both Balance columns opposite the closing entry.
6. Prepare a post-closing trial balance.

DOS Instructions

1. Load the General Ledger Software program (IA1) from the program disk.

   Key **IA1** and press Enter at the DOS prompt. To the question "Read About General Ledger Software?" select **No** to bypass the copyright screens.

2. Load the file **04-5B** from the program disk.

   Press the **Alt** key to activate menu selection. Choose the **Open Accounting File** command in the File menu. Select the **Files** button and choose the accounting file to open. Select the Ok button to open the file.

3. Carefully key your name in the Student Name field in the General Information window. Press Ctrl+Enter to select Ok.

4. Choose the **Save As** command in the File menu and save the file to the drive and directory containing your data files. Key a file name of XXX4-5B (where XXX are your initials). Press Ctrl+Enter to select Ok.

5. Key the adjusting entries in the General Journal.

   Key 2000 as the current year and enter 03/31 as the date for each entry. Key the letter for each adjusting entry in the Reference field; for example, (a), (b), etc. To display a list of accounts, press the F1 key. After each entry is keyed, press Ctrl+Enter to select Ok. When the Posting Summary window appears, press Ctrl+Enter to Post.

6. Display the adjusting entries.

Select **Journals** from the Reports menu and select **General Journal** in the Report Selection window. Select the Ok button in the Selection Options window to display the adjusting entries. Press the F9 key to print the general journal report.

7. Make corrections to the adjusting entries, if necessary.

Select **List** in the General Journal window to display the adjusting entries. Select the entry for correction and make the necessary change(s).

8. Display the income statement, balance sheet, and statement of owner's equity.

Select **Financial Statements** from the Reports menu and select **Income Statement, Balance Sheet,** and **Statement of Owner's Equity** in the Report Selection window. Press the F9 key to print the financial statements.

9. Choose the **Save Accounting File** command in the File menu.

10. Perform period-end closing.

Choose **Period-End Closing** from the Options menu. When the dialog box appears, press Ctrl+Enter to select Ok.

11. Display a post-closing trial balance.

Select **Ledgers** from the Reports menu and select **Trial Balance** in the Report Selection window. Press the F9 key to print the trial balance report.

12. Choose the **Save As** command in the File menu to save your data file. Key a file name of XXX4-5BP (where XXX are your initials, 4-5B represents the problem number, and P represents post closing). Press Ctrl+Enter to select Ok.

Windows Instructions

To access Help, click on the Help button that appears in most windows.

1. Click on the **Open** toolbar button and double-click on 04-5B to open the file.

2. Carefully key your name in the User Name field and click on the OK button.

3. Click on the **Save As** toolbar button and save the file to the drive and directory containing your data files. Key a file name of XXX4-5B (where XXX are your initials). Click on the OK button.

4. Click on the **Journal** toolbar button and key the adjusting entries in the General Journal.

Key 03/31/00 as the date for each entry. Key the letter for each adjusting entry in the Reference field: for example, (a), (b), etc. After each entry is keyed, click on the **Post** button (or press Enter).

5. Display the adjusting entries.

Click on the **Reports** toolbar button and click on **Journals** in the Report Selection window. Click on **General Journal** and the OK button to choose a report to display. Click on **Include All Journal Entries** and the OK button to display the adjusting entries report. To print the report, click on the **Print** button.

6. Make corrections to the adjusting entries, if necessary.

In the General Journal window, click on the entry to correct, then key the correction(s) to the journal entry and click on the **Post** button (or press Enter).

7. Display the income statement, balance sheet, and statement of owner's equity.

Click on the **Reports** toolbar button and click on **Financial Statements**. Click on **Income Statement, Balance Sheet,** and **Statement of Owner's Equity** in the Report Selection window. To print each report, click on the **Print** button.

8. Click on the **Save** toolbar button to save your file.

9. Click on **Generate Closing Journal Entries** in the Options menu. When the dialog box appears, click on the **Yes** button. When the closing entries appear, click on the **Post** button.

10. Display a post-closing trial balance.

Click on the **Reports** toolbar button and click on **Ledger Reports**. Click on **Trial Balance** and the OK button to choose a report to display. To print the report, click on the **Print** button.

11. Click on the **Save As** toolbar button to save your data file. Key a file name of XXX4-5BP (where XXX are your initials, 4-5B represents the problem number, and P represents post closing). Click on the OK button.

Comprehensive Problem 1

For the past several years, Angie Mills has operated a part-time consulting business from her home. As of September 1, 2000, Angie decided to move to rented quarters and to operate the business, which was to be known as Interactive Consulting, on a full-time basis. Interactive Consulting entered into the following transactions during September:

Sept. 1. The following assets were received from Angie Mills: cash, $7,050; accounts receivable, $1,500; supplies, $1,250; and office equipment, $7,200. There were no liabilities received.
2. Paid three months' rent on a lease rental contract, $3,600.
2. Paid the premiums on property and casualty insurance policies, $1,500.
4. Received cash from clients as an advance payment for services to be provided and recorded it as unearned fees, $3,500.
5. Purchased additional office equipment on account from Payne Company, $1,800.
6. Received cash from clients on account, $800.
10. Paid cash for a newspaper advertisement, $120.
12. Paid Payne Company for part of the debt incurred on September 5, $800.
12. Recorded services provided on account for the period September 1–12, $1,200.
13. Paid part-time receptionist for two weeks' salary, $400.
17. Recorded cash from cash clients for fees earned during the first half of September, $2,100.
18. Paid cash for supplies, $750.
20. Recorded services provided on account for the period September 13–20, $1,100.
24. Recorded cash from cash clients for fees earned for the period September 17–24, $1,850.
25. Received cash from clients on account, $1,300.
27. Paid part-time receptionist for two weeks' salary, $400.
29. Paid telephone bill for September, $130.
30. Paid electricity bill for September, $200.
30. Recorded cash from cash clients for fees earned for the period September 25–30, $1,050.
30. Recorded services provided on account for the remainder of September, $500.
30. Angie withdrew $1,500 for personal use.

Instructions

1. Journalize each transaction in a two-column journal, referring to the following chart of accounts in selecting the accounts to be debited and credited. (Do not insert the account numbers in the journal at this time.)

11	Cash	31	Angie Mills, Capital
12	Accounts Receivable	32	Angie Mills, Drawing
14	Supplies	41	Fees Earned
15	Prepaid Rent	51	Salary Expense
16	Prepaid Insurance	52	Rent Expense
18	Office Equipment	53	Supplies Expense
19	Accumulated Depreciation	54	Depreciation Expense
21	Accounts Payable	55	Insurance Expense
22	Salaries Payable	59	Miscellaneous Expense
23	Unearned Fees		

2. Post the journal to a ledger of four-column accounts.
3. Prepare a trial balance as of September 30, 2000, on a ten-column work sheet, listing all the accounts in the order given in the ledger. Complete the work sheet, using the following adjustment data:
   a. Insurance expired during September is $125.
   b. Supplies on hand on September 30 are $1,220.
   c. Depreciation of office equipment for September is $250.

      d. Accrued receptionist salary on September 30 is $120.

      e. Rent expired during September is $800.

      f. Unearned fees on September 30 are $1,200.

4. Prepare an income statement, a statement of owner's equity, and a balance sheet.

5. Journalize and post the adjusting entries.

6. Journalize and post the closing entries. (Income Summary is account #33 in the chart of accounts.) Indicate closed accounts by inserting a line in both Balance columns opposite the closing entry.

7. Prepare a post-closing trial balance.

DOS Instructions

1. Load the General Ledger Software program (IA1) from the program disk.

    Key **IA1** and press Enter at the DOS prompt. To the question "Read About General Ledger Software?" select **No** to bypass the copyright screens.

2. Load the file **C-1** from the program disk.

    Press the **Alt** key to activate menu selection. Choose the **Open Accounting File** command in the File menu. Select the **Files** button and choose the accounting file to open. Select the Ok button to open the file.

3. Carefully key your name in the Student Name field in the General Information window. Press Ctrl+Enter to select Ok.

4. Choose the **Save As** command in the File menu and save the file to the drive and directory containing your data files. Key a file name of XXXC-1 (where XXX are your initials). Press Ctrl+Enter to select Ok.

5. Key the journal entries in the General Journal.

    Type 2000 as the current year and enter the date for each transaction. Leave the Reference field blank. To display a list of accounts, press the F1 key. After each journal entry is keyed, press Ctrl+Enter to select Ok. When the Posting Summary window appears, press Ctrl+Enter to Post.

6. Display the journal entries.

    Select **Journals** from the Reports menu and select **General Journal** in the Report Selection window. Select the Ok button in the Selection Options window to display the journal entries for September. Press the F9 key to print the general journal report.

7. Make corrections to the journal entries, if necessary.

    Select **List** in the General Journal window to display the journal entries. Select the entry for correction and make the necessary change(s).

8. Display a trial balance.

    Select **Ledgers** from the Reports menu and select **Trial Balance** in the Report Selection window. Press the F9 key to print the trial balance report.

9. Key the adjusting entries in the General Journal.

    Type 2000 as the current year and enter 09/30 as the date for each entry. Key Adj.Ent. in the Reference field. To display a list of accounts, press the F1 key. After each entry is keyed, press Ctrl+Enter to select Ok. When the Posting Summary window appears, press Ctrl+Enter to Post.

10. Display the adjusting entries.

    Select **Journals** from the Reports menu and select **General Journal** in the Report Selection window. Key Adj.Ent. in the Reference restriction field of the Selection Options window. Press the Ok button to display the adjusting entries. Press the F9 key to print the general journal report.

11. Make corrections to the adjusting entries, if necessary.

    Select **List** in the General Journal window to display the adjusting entries. Select the entry for correction and make the necessary change(s).

12. Display the income statement, balance sheet, and statement of owner's equity.

Select **Financial Statements** from the Reports menu and select **Income Statement, Balance Sheet,** and **Statement of Owner's Equity** in the Report Selection window. Press the F9 key to print each report.

13. Choose the **Save Accounting File** command in the File menu.

14. Perform period-end closing.

    Choose **Period-End Closing** from the Options menu. When the dialog box appears, press Ctrl+Enter to select Ok.

15. Display a post-closing trial balance.

    Select **Ledgers** from the Reports menu and select **Trial Balance** in the Report Selection window. Press the F9 key to print the trial balance report.

16. Choose the **Save As** command in the File menu to save your data file. Key a file name of XXXC-1P (where XXX are your initials, C-1 represents the problem number, and P represents post closing). Press Ctrl+Enter to select Ok.

Windows Instructions

To access Help, click on the Help button that appears in most windows.

1. Click on the **Open** toolbar button and double-click on C-1 to open the file.

2. Carefully key your name in the User Name field and click on the OK button.

3. Click on the **Save As** toolbar button and save the file to the drive and directory containing your data files. Key a file name of XXXC-1 (where XXX are your initials). Click on the OK button.

4. Click on the **Journal** toolbar button and key the journal entries in the General Journal.

    Key the date for each transaction. Leave the Reference field blank. After each journal entry is keyed, click on the **Post** button (or press Enter).

5. Display the journal entries.

    Click on the **Reports** toolbar button and click on **Journals** in the Report Selection window. Click on **General Journal** and the OK button to choose a report to display. Click on **Include All Journal Entries** and the OK button to display the general journal report. To print the report, click on the **Print** button.

6. Make corrections to the journal entries, if necessary.

    In the General Journal window, click on the entry to correct, then key the correction(s) to the journal entry and click on the **Post** button (or press Enter).

7. Display a trial balance.

    Click on the **Reports** toolbar button and click on **Ledger Reports**. Click on **Trial Balance** and the OK button to choose a report to display. To print the report, click on the **Print** button.

8. Key the adjusting entries in the General Journal.

    Key 09/30/00 as the date for each entry. Key Adj.Ent. in the Reference field. After each entry is keyed, click on the **Post** button (or press Enter).

9. Display the adjusting entries.

    Click on the **Reports** toolbar button and click on **Journals** in the Report Selection window. Click on **General Journal** and the OK button to choose a report to display. Click on **Customize Journal Report** and select **Adj.Ent.** in the Reference drop-down list. Click on the OK button to display the adjusting entries report. To print the report, click on the **Print** button.

10. Make corrections to the adjusting entries, if necessary.

    In the General Journal window, click on the entry to correct, then key the correction(s) to the journal entry and click on the **Post** button (or press Enter).

11. Display the income statement, balance sheet, and statement of owner's equity.

Click on the **Reports** toolbar button and click on **Financial Statements**. Click on **Income Statement, Balance Sheet,** and **Statement of Owner's Equity**. To print each report, click on the **Print** button.

12. Click on the **Save** toolbar button to save your file.

13. Click on **Generate Closing Journal Entries** in the Options menu. When the dialog box appears, click on the **Yes** button. When the closing entries appear, click on the **Post** button.

14. Display a post-closing trial balance.

   Click on the **Reports** toolbar button and click on **Ledger Reports**. Click on **Trial Balance** and the OK button to choose a report to display. To print the report, click on the **Print** button.

15. Click on the **Save As** toolbar button to save your data file. Key a file name of XXXC-1P (where XXX are your initials, C-1 represents the problem number, and P represents post closing). Click on the OK button.

Problem 5–5A
All journals and general ledger; trial balance
Objective 3

The transactions completed by Same-Day Courier Company during May, the first month of the fiscal year, were as follows:

May
1. Issued Check No. 205 for May rent, $1,000.
2. Purchased a vehicle on account from Bunting Co., $24,500.
3. Purchased office equipment on account from Gill Computer Co., $4,600.
5. Issued Invoice No. 91 to Carlton Co., $1,600.
6. Received check for $4,200 from Pease Co. in payment of invoice.
6. Issued Check No. 206 for fuel expense, $800.
9. Issued Invoice No. 92 to Collins Co., $2,340.
10. Received check for $8,150 from Sing Co. in payment of invoice.
10. Issued Check No. 207 to Haber Enterprises in payment of $3,160 invoice.
10. Issued Check No. 208 to Bastille Co. in payment of $2,000 invoice.
11. Issued Invoice No. 93 to Joy Co., $950.
11. Issued Check No. 209 to Porter Co. in payment of $910 invoice.
12. Received check for $1,600 from Carlton Co. in payment of invoice.
13. Issued Check No. 210 to Bunting Co. in payment of $24,500 invoice.
16. Cash fees earned for May 1–16, $14,450.
16. Issued Check No. 211 for purchase of a vehicle, $12,000.
17. Purchased maintenance supplies on account from Bastille Co., $3,150.
18. Issued Check No. 212 for miscellaneous administrative expenses, $1,900.
18. Received check for rent revenue on office space, $1,100.
19. Purchased the following on account from Master Co.: maintenance supplies, $1,500, and office supplies, $2,500.
20. Issued Check No. 213 in payment of advertising expense, $1,350.
20. Used maintenance supplies with a cost of $3,900 to overhaul vehicle engines.
23. Issued Invoice No. 94 to Sing Co., $4,200.
24. Purchased office supplies on account from Haber Enterprises, $700.
25. Received check for $2,150 from Pease Co. in payment of invoice.
25. Issued Invoice No. 95 to Collins Co., $6,700.
26. Issued Check No. 214 to Gill Computer Co. in payment of $4,600 invoice.
27. Issued Check No. 215 to C. Davis as a personal withdrawal, $3,200.
30. Issued Check No. 216 in payment of driver salaries, $14,600.
31. Issued Check No. 217 in payment of office salaries, $6,700.
31. Issued Check No. 218 for office supplies, $720.
31. Cash fees earned for May 17–31, $18,600.

Instructions

1. Enter the following account balances in the general ledger as of May 1:

11	Cash	$ 28,400	32	C. Davis, Drawing	—
12	Accounts Receivable	14,500	41	Fees Earned	—
14	Maintenance Supplies	5,200	42	Rent Revenue	—
15	Office Supplies	3,400	51	Driver Salaries Expense	—
16	Office Equipment	16,800	52	Maintenance Supplies	
17	Accumulated Depreciation—			Expense	—
	Office Equipment	4,100	53	Fuel Expense	—
18	Vehicles	82,000	61	Office Salaries Expense	—
19	Accumulated Depreciation—		62	Rent Expense	—
	Vehicles	16,300	63	Advertising Expense	—
21	Accounts Payable	6,070	64	Miscellaneous Administrative	
31	C. Davis, Capital	123,830		Expense	—

2. Journalize the transactions for May 2000 using the following journals similar to those illustrated in this chapter: single-column revenue journal, cash receipts journal, purchases journal (with columns for Accounts Payable, Maintenance Supplies, Office Supplies, and Other Accounts), cash payments journal, and two-column general journal. You do not need to make daily postings to the individual accounts in the accounts payable ledger and the accounts receivable ledger.
3. Post the appropriate individual entries to the general ledger.
4. Total each of the columns of the special journals, and post the appropriate totals to the general ledger; insert the account balances.
5. Prepare a trial balance.
6. Verify the agreement of each subsidiary ledger with its controlling account. The sum of the balances of the accounts in the subsidiary ledgers as of May 31 are as follows:

Accounts receivable $14,190
Accounts payable   7,850

DOS Instructions

1. Load the General Ledger Software program (IA1) from the program disk.

   Key **IA1** and press Enter at the DOS prompt. To the question "Read About General Ledger Software?" select **No** to bypass the copyright screens.

2. Load the file **05-5A** from the program disk.

   Press the **Alt** key to activate menu selection. Choose the **Open Accounting File** command in the File menu. Select the **Files** button and choose the accounting file to open. Select the Ok button to open the file.

3. Carefully key your name in the Student Name field in the General Information window. Press Ctrl+Enter to select Ok.

4. Choose the **Save As** command in the File menu and save the file to the drive and directory containing your data files. Key a file name of XXX5-5A (where XXX are your initials). Press Ctrl+Enter to select Ok.

5. Key the journal entries in the appropriate journals. Choose the appropriate journal from the Journals menu. After each journal entry is keyed, press Ctrl+Enter to select Ok. When the Posting Summary appears, press Ctrl+Enter to Post.

   In the **General Journal**, type 2000 as the current year and key the date for each transaction. Leave the Reference field blank. To display a list of accounts, press the F1 key.

   In the **Purchases Journal**, for each entry, type 2000 as the current year and key the date for each transaction and the vendor number. Press the F2 key to display a vendor list. Leave the invoice number field blank. Key the invoice amount. Key the account numbers and debit amounts. The entry to Accounts Payable Credit is automatically made by the computer.

   In the **Cash Payments Journal**, for each entry, type 2000 as the current year and key the date for each transaction and the check number. When appropriate, key the vendor number and the amount in the Accts. Pay. Debit field. Otherwise, key the other debit entries. Press the F2 key to display a vendor list. The entry to Cash Credit is automatically made by the computer.

In the **Sales Journal**, for each entry, type 2000 as the current year and key the date for each transaction, the customer number, invoice number and invoice amount. Press the F3 key to display a customer list. Key the account number and amount of the credit entry. The entry to Accts. Receivable Debit is automatically made by the computer.

In the **Cash Receipts Journal**, type 2000 as the current year and key the date for each transaction. Leave the Reference field blank. When appropriate, key the customer number and the amount in the Accts. Receivable Credit field. Otherwise, key the other credit entries. Press the F3 key to display a customer list. The entry to Cash Debit is automatically made by the computer.

6. Display the journal entries.

   Select **Journals** from the Reports menu and select **General Journal, Purchases Journal, Cash Payments Journal, Sales Journal,** and **Cash Receipts Journal** in the Report Selection window. Select the Ok button in the Selection Options window to display the journal entries for May. Press the F9 key to print each journal report.

7. Make corrections to the journal entries, if necessary.

   Select **List** in the appropriate journal window to display the journal entries. Select the entry for correction and make the necessary change(s).

8. Display a trial balance.

   Select **Ledgers** from the Reports menu and select **Trial Balance** in the Report Selection window. Press the F9 key to print the trial balance report.

9. Display a schedule of accounts payable and a schedule of accounts receivable.

   Select **Ledgers** from the Reports menu and select **Schedule of Accounts Payable** and **Schedule of Accounts Receivable** in the Report Selection window. Press the F9 key to print each report.

10. Choose the **Save Accounting File** command in the File menu to save your data file.

Windows Instructions

To access Help, click on the Help button that appears in most windows.

1. Click on the **Open** toolbar button and double-click on 05-5A to open the file.

2. Carefully key your name in the User Name field and click on the OK button.

3. Click on the **Save As** toolbar button and save the file to the drive and directory containing your data files. Key a file name of XXX5-5A (where XXX are your initials). Click on the OK button.

4. Click on the **Journal** toolbar button and click on the appropriate journal tab to key the entries into the special journals. Key the date for each transaction. After each journal entry is keyed, click on the **Post** button (or press Enter).

   In the **General Journal**, leave the Reference field blank.

   In the **Purchases Journal**, leave the Refer. field blank. Key the account numbers and debit amounts. The credit entry to Accounts Payable is automatically made by the computer. Key the vendor name (or select the vendor name from the drop-down list).

   In the **Cash Payments Journal**, for each entry, key the check number in the Refer. field. Key the debit entries and the entries to Accounts Payable. When appropriate, key the vendor name (or select the vendor name from the drop-down list). The credit entry to Cash is automatically made by the computer.

   In the **Sales Journal**, for each entry, key the invoice number in the Refer. field. Key the amount in the Fees Credit column. The entry to Accounts Receivable Debit is automatically made by the computer. Key the customer name (or select the customer name from the drop-down list).

   In the **Cash Receipts Journal**, for each entry, leave the Refer. field blank. Key the credit entries and the entries to Accounts Receivable. When appropriate, key the customer name (or select the customer name from the drop-down list).

5. Display the journal entries.

    Click on the **Reports** toolbar button and click on **Journals** in the Report Selection window. Click on **General Journal, Purchases Journal, Cash Payments Journal, Sales Journal,** and **Cash Receipts Journal** and the OK button to choose a report to display. Click on **Include All Journal Entries** and the OK button to display the journal reports. To print each report, click on the **Print** button.

6. Make corrections to the journal entries, if necessary.

    In the journals window, click on the entry to correct, then key the correction(s) to the journal entry and click on the **Post** button (or press Enter).

7. Display a trial balance, schedule of accounts payable, and schedule of accounts receivable.

    Click on the **Reports** toolbar button and click on **Ledger Reports**. Click **on Trial Balance, Schedule of Accounts Payable,** and **Schedule of Accounts Receivable**. To print each report, click on the **Print** button.

8. Click on the **Save** toolbar button to save your data file.

Problem 5–5B
All journals and general ledger; trial balance
Objective 3

The transactions completed by Speedy Delivery Company during July, the first month of the fiscal year, were as follows:

July   1. Issued Check No. 610 for July rent, $1,000.
        2. Issued Invoice No. 940 to Capps Co., $2,000.
        3. Received check for $6,700 from Pease Co. in payment of invoice.
        5. Purchased a vehicle on account from Browning Transportation, $21,300.
        6. Purchased office equipment on account from Gunter Computer Co., $4,200.
        6. Issued Invoice No. 941 to Collins Co., $3,500.
        9. Issued Check No. 611 for fuel expense, $900.
       10. Received check from Sokol Co. in payment of $4,400 invoice.
       10. Issued Check No. 612 for $4,200 to Hoy Co. in payment of invoice.
       10. Issued Invoice No. 942 to Joy Co., $6,600.
       11. Issued Check No. 613 to Burks Co. in payment of $2,300 invoice.
       11. Issued Check No. 614 for $1,500 to Porter Co. in payment of account.
       12. Received check from Capps Co. in payment of $2,000 invoice.
       13. Issued Check No. 615 to Browning Transportation in payment of $21,300 balance.
       16. Issued Check No. 616 for $9,000 for cash purchase of a vehicle.
       16. Cash fees earned for July 1–16, $10,600.
       17. Issued Check No. 617 for miscellaneous administrative expense, $1,200.
       18. Purchased maintenance supplies on account from Burks Co., $1,200.
       19. Purchased the following on account from McClain Co.: maintenance supplies, $1,450; office supplies, $1,750.
       20. Issued Check No. 618 in payment of advertising expense, $1,400.
       20. Used $3,200 maintenance supplies to repair delivery vehicles.
       23. Purchased office supplies on account from Hoy Co., $500.
       24. Issued Invoice No. 943 to Sokol Co., $5,700.
       24. Issued Check No. 619 to D. D. Miles as a personal withdrawal, $4,000.
       25. Issued Invoice No. 944 to Collins Co., $9,300.
       25. Received check for $7,200 from Pease Co. in payment of balance.
       26. Issued Check No. 620 to Gunter Computer Co. in payment of $4,200 invoice of July 3.
       30. Issued Check No. 621 for monthly salaries as follows: driver salaries, $12,000; office salaries, $8,000.
       31. Cash fees earned for July 17–31, $7,400.
       31. Issued Check No. 622 in payment for office supplies, $700.
       31. Received check for rent revenue on office space, $500.

Instructions

1. Enter the following account balances in the general ledger as of July 1:

11	Cash	$ 36,800	32	D. D. Miles, Drawing	—
12	Accounts Receivable	18,300	41	Fees Earned	—
14	Maintenance Supplies	5,400	42	Rent Revenue	—
15	Office Supplies	3,600	51	Driver Salaries Expense	—
16	Office Equipment	18,900	52	Maintenance Supplies	
17	Accumulated Depreciation—			Expense	—
	Office Equipment	2,200	53	Fuel Expense	—
18	Vehicles	56,000	61	Office Salaries Expense	—
19	Accumulated Depreciation—		62	Rent Expense	—
	Vehicles	8,800	63	Advertising Expense	—
21	Accounts Payable	8,000	64	Miscellaneous Administrative	
31	D. D. Miles, Capital	120,000		Expense	—

2. Journalize the transactions for July 2000 using the following journals similar to those illustrated in this chapter: cash receipts journal, purchases journal (with columns for Accounts Payable, Maintenance Supplies, Office Supplies, and Other Accounts), single-column revenue journal, cash payments journal, and two-column general journal. You do not need to make daily postings to the individual accounts in the accounts payable ledger and the accounts receivable ledger.
3. Post the appropriate individual entries to the general ledger.
4. Total each of the columns of the special journals and post the appropriate totals to the general ledger; insert the account balances.
5. Prepare a trial balance.
6. Verify the agreement of each subsidiary ledger with its controlling account. The sum of the balances of the accounts in the subsidiary ledgers as of July 31 are:

Accounts receivable	$25,100
Accounts payable	4,900

DOS Instructions

1. Load the General Ledger Software program (IA1) from the program disk.

   Key **IA1** and press Enter at the DOS prompt. To the question "Read About General Ledger Software?" select **No** to bypass the copyright screens.

2. Load the file **05-5B** from the program disk.

   Press the **Alt** key to activate menu selection. Choose the **Open Accounting File** command in the File menu. Select the **Files** button and choose the accounting file to open. Select the Ok button to open the file.

3. Carefully key your name in the Student Name field in the General Information window. Press Ctrl+Enter to select Ok.

4. Choose the **Save As** command in the File menu and save the file to the drive and directory containing your data files. Key a file name of XXX5-5B (where XXX are your initials). Press Ctrl+Enter to select Ok.

5. Key the journal entries in the appropriate journals. Choose the appropriate journal from the Journals menu. After each journal entry is keyed, press Ctrl+Enter to select Ok. When the Posting Summary appears, press Ctrl+Enter to Post.

   In the **General Journal**, type 2000 as the current year and key the date for each transaction. Leave the Reference field blank. To display a list of accounts, press the F1 key.

   In the **Purchases Journal**, for each entry, type 2000 as the current year and key the date for each transaction and the vendor number. Press the F2 key to display a vendor list. Leave the invoice number field blank. Key the invoice amount. Key the account numbers and debit amounts. The entry to Accounts Payable Credit is automatically made by the computer.

   In the **Cash Payments Journal**, for each entry, type 2000 as the current year and key the date for each transaction and the check number. When appropriate, key the vendor number and the amount in the Accts. Pay. Debit field. Otherwise, key the other debit entries. Press the F2 key to display a vendor list. The entry to Cash Credit is automatically made by the computer.

In the **Sales Journal**, for each entry, type 2000 as the current year and key the date for each transaction, the customer number, invoice number and invoice amount. Press the F3 key to display a customer list. Key the account number and amount of the credit entry. The entry to Accts. Receivable Debit is automatically made by the computer.

In the **Cash Receipts Journal**, type 2000 as the current year and key the date for each transaction. Leave the Reference field blank. When appropriate, key the customer number and the amount in the Accts. Receivable Credit field. Otherwise, key the other credit entries. Press the F3 key to display a customer list. The entry to Cash Debit is automatically made by the computer.

6. Display the journal entries.

   Select **Journals** from the Reports menu and select **General Journal, Purchases Journal, Cash Payments Journal, Sales Journal,** and **Cash Receipts Journal** in the Report Selection window. Select the Ok button in the Selection Options window to display the journal entries for July. Press the F9 key to print each journal report.

7. Make corrections to the journal entries, if necessary.

   Select **List** in the appropriate journal window to display the journal entries. Select the entry for correction and make the necessary change(s).

8. Display a trial balance.

   Select **Ledgers** from the Reports menu and select **Trial Balance** in the Report Selection window. Press the F9 key to print the trial balance report.

9. Display a schedule of accounts payable and a schedule of accounts receivable.

   Select **Ledgers** from the Reports menu and select **Schedule of Accounts Payable** and **Schedule of Accounts Receivable** in the Report Selection window. Press the F9 key to print each report.

10. Choose the **Save Accounting File** command in the File menu to save your data file.

Windows Instructions   **To access Help, click on the Help button that appears in most windows.**

1. Click on the **Open** toolbar button and double-click on 05-5B to open the file.

2. Carefully key your name in the User Name field and click on the OK button.

3. Click on the **Save As** toolbar button and save the file to the drive and directory containing your data files. Key a file name of XXX5-5B (where XXX are your initials). Click on the OK button.

4. Click on the **Journal** toolbar button and click on the appropriate journal tab to key the entries into the special journals. Key the date for each transaction. After each journal entry is keyed, click on the **Post** button (or press Enter).

   In the **General Journal**, leave the Reference field blank.

   In the **Purchases Journal**, leave the Refer. field blank. Key the account numbers and debit amounts. The credit entry to Accounts Payable is automatically made by the computer. Key the vendor name (or select the vendor name from the drop-down list).

   In the **Cash Payments Journal**, for each entry, key the check number in the Refer. field. Key the debit entries and the entries to Accounts Payable. When appropriate, key the vendor name (or select the vendor name from the drop-down list). The credit entry to Cash is automatically made by the computer.

   In the **Sales Journal**, for each entry, key the invoice number in the Refer. field. Key the amount in the Fees Credit column. The entry to Accounts Receivable Debit is automatically made by the computer. Key the customer name (or select the customer name from the drop-down list).

   In the **Cash Receipts Journal**, for each entry, leave the Refer. field blank. Key the credit entries and the entries to Accounts Receivable. When appropriate, key the customer name (or select the customer name from the drop-down list). The debit entry to Cash is automatically made by the computer.

5. Display the journal entries.

   Click on the **Reports** toolbar button and click on **Journals** in the Report Selection window. Click on **General Journal, Purchases Journal, Cash Payments Journal, Sales Journal,** and **Cash Receipts Journal** and the OK button to choose a report to display. Click on **Include All Journal Entries** and the OK button to display the journal reports. To print each report, click on the **Print** button.

6. Make corrections to the journal entries, if necessary.

   In the journals window, click on the entry to correct, then key the correction(s) to the journal entry and click on the **Post** button (or press Enter).

7. Display the trial balance, schedule of accounts payable, and schedule of accounts receivable.

   Click on the **Reports** toolbar button and click on **Ledger Reports**. Click **on Trial Balance, Schedule of Accounts Payable,** and **Schedule of Accounts Receivable**. To print each report, click on the **Print** button.

8. Click on the **Save** toolbar button to save your data file.

Problem 6–3A
Sales-related and purchase-related transactions
Objective 2

The accounts and their balances in the ledger of Taxel Company on March 1 of the current year are as follows:

Cash..	$17,544
Accounts Receivable..	9,500
Merchandise Inventory...	76,095
Prepaid Insurance...	3,200
Office Supplies...	1,000
Accounts Payable	12,000
Roberta Stevens, Capital	84,660
Roberta Stevens, Drawing	16,000
Sales...	77,300
Sales Returns & Allowances	5,500
Sales Discounts	666
Cost of Merchandise Sold....................................	16,245
Sales Salaries Expense	10,500
Advertising Expense	5,000
Credit Card Expense...	260
Miscellaneous Selling Expense.............................	250
Office Salaries Expense.......................................	6,500
Rent Expense...	5,500
Miscellaneous Administrative Expense...................	200

The following were selected from among the transactions completed by Taxel Company during March of the current year:

Mar. 2. Purchased merchandise on account from Queen Co., list price $25,000, trade discount 30%, terms FOB shipping point, 2/10, n/30, with prepaid transportation costs of $720 added to the invoice.

4. Purchased merchandise on account from Rossi Co., $6,000, terms FOB destination, 1/10, n/30.

6. Sold merchandise on account to C. F. Howell Co., list price $7,500, trade discount 40%, terms 2/10, n/30. The cost of the merchandise sold was $1,850.

9. Returned $1,300 of merchandise purchased on March 4 from Rossi Co.

12. Paid Queen Co. on account for purchase of March 2, less discount.

14. Paid Rossi Co. on account for purchase of March 4, less return of March 9 and discount.

16. Received cash on account from sale of March 6 to C. F. Howell Co., less discount.

19. Sold merchandise on nonbank credit cards and reported accounts to the card company, American Express, $4,450. The cost of the merchandise sold was $2,950.

22. Sold merchandise on account to Vantage Co., $3,480, terms 2/10, n/30. The cost of the merchandise sold was $1,400.

24. Sold merchandise for cash, $4,350. The cost of the merchandise sold was $1,750.

Mar. 25. Received merchandise returned by Vantage Co. from sale on March 22, $1,480. The cost of the returned merchandise was $600.

       31. Received cash from American Express for nonbank credit card sales of March 19, less $290 service fee.

Instructions

Journalize the transactions.

DOS Instructions

1. Load the General Ledger Software program (IA1) from the program disk.

   Key **IA1** and press Enter at the DOS prompt. To the question "Read About General Ledger Software?" select **No** to bypass the copyright screens.

2. Load the file **06-3A** from the program disk.

   Press the **Alt** key to activate menu selection. Choose the **Open Accounting File** command in the File menu. Select the **Files** button and choose the accounting file to open. Select the Ok button to open the file.

3. Carefully key your name in the Student Name field in the General Information window. Press Ctrl+Enter to select Ok.

4. Choose the **Save As** command in the File menu and save the file to the drive and directory containing your data files. Key a file name of XXX6-3A (where XXX are your initials). Press Ctrl+Enter to select Ok.

5. Key the journal entries in the General Journal.

   Key the date for each transaction. Leave the Reference field blank. To display a list of accounts, press the F1 key. To display lists of vendors or customers, press the F2 and F3 keys, respectively. After each journal entry is keyed, press Ctrl+Enter to select Ok. When the Posting Summary window appears, press Ctrl+Enter to Post.

6. Display the journal entries.

   Select **Journals** from the Reports menu and select **General Journal** in the Report Selection window. Select the Ok button in the Selection Options window to display the journal entries for March. Press the F9 key to print the general journal report.

7. Make corrections to the journal entries, if necessary.

   Select **List** in the General Journal window to display the journal entries. Select the entry for correction and make the necessary change(s).

8. Display a trial balance.

   Select **Ledgers** from the Reports menu and select **Trial Balance** in the Report Selection window. Press the F9 key to print the trial balance report.

9. Key the adjusting entries in the General Journal based on the following data:

Insurance expired on March 31	$400.00
Office supplies on hand on March 31	$300.00

   Type the current year and enter 03/31 as the date for each entry. Key Adj.Ent. in the Reference field. To display a list of accounts, press the F1 key. After each entry is keyed, press Ctrl+Enter to select Ok. When the Posting Summary window appears, press Ctrl+Enter to Post.

10. Display the adjusting entries.

    Select **Journals** from the Reports menu and select **General Journal** in the Report Selection window. Key **Adj.Ent.** in the Reference restriction field of the Selection Options window. Press the Ok button to display the adjusting entries. Press the F9 key to print the general journal report.

11. Make corrections to the adjusting entries, if necessary.

    Select **List** in the General Journal window to display the adjusting entries. Select the entry for correction and make the necessary change(s).

12. Display the income statement, balance sheet, and statement of owner's equity.

    Select **Financial Statements** from the Reports menu and select **Income Statement, Balance Sheet,** and **Statement of Owner's Equity** in the Report Selection window. Press the F9 key to print each report.

13. Choose the **Save Accounting File** command in the File menu.

14. Perform period-end closing.

    Choose **Period-End Closing** from the Options menu. When the dialog box appears, press Ctrl+Enter to select Ok.

15. Display a post-closing trial balance.

    Select **Ledgers** from the Reports menu and select **Trial Balance** in the Report Selection window. Press the F9 key to print the trial balance report.

16. Choose the **Save As** command in the File menu to save your data file. Key a file name of XXX6-3AP (where XXX are your initials, 6-3A represents the problem number, and P represents post closing). Press Ctrl+Enter to select Ok.

Windows Instructions

To access Help, click on the Help button that appears in most windows.

1. Click on the **Open** toolbar button and double-click on 06-3A to open the file.

2. Carefully key your name in the User Name field and click on the OK button.

3. Click on the **Save As** toolbar button and save the file to the drive and directory containing your data files. Key a file name of XXX6-3A (where XXX are your initials). Click on the OK button.

4. Click on the **Journal** toolbar button and key the journal entries in the General Journal.

   Key the date for each transaction. Leave the Reference field blank. When appropriate, key the vendor/customer name (or select the vendor/customer name from the drop-down list). After each journal entry is keyed, click on the **Post** button (or press Enter).

5. Display the journal entries.

   Click on the **Reports** toolbar button and click on **Journals** in the Report Selection window. Click on **General Journal** and the OK button to choose a report to display. Click on **Include All Journal Entries** and the OK button to display the general journal report. To print the report, click on the **Print** button.

6. Make corrections to the journal entries, if necessary.

   In the General Journal window, click on the entry to correct, then key the correction(s) to the journal entry and click on the **Post** button (or press Enter).

7. Display a trial balance.

   Click on the **Reports** toolbar button and click on **Ledger Reports**. Click on **Trial Balance** and the OK button to choose a report to display. To print the report, click on the **Print** button.

8. Key the adjusting entries in the General Journal based on the following data:

Insurance expired on March 31	$400.00
Office supplies on hand on March 31	$300.00

   Key 03/31/-- (where -- is the current year) for each entry. Key **Adj.Ent.** in the Reference field. After each entry is keyed, click on the **Post** button (or press Enter).

9. Display the adjusting entries.

   Click on the **Reports** toolbar button and click on **Journals** in the Report Selection window. Click on **General Journal** and the OK button to choose a report to display. Click on **Customize Journal Report** and select **Adj.Ent.** in the Reference drop-down list. Click on the OK button to display the adjusting entries report. To print the report, click on the **Print** button.

10. Make corrections to the adjusting entries, if necessary.

In the General Journal window, click on the entry to correct, then key the correction(s) to the journal entry and click on the **Post** button (or press Enter).

11. Display the income statement, balance sheet, and statement of owner's equity.

    Click on the **Reports** toolbar button and click on **Financial Statements**. Click on **Income Statement, Balance Sheet,** and **Statement of Owner's Equity.** To print each report, click on the **Print** button.

12. Click on the **Save** toolbar button to save your file.

13. Click on **Generate Closing Journal Entries** in the Options menu. When the dialog box appears, click on the **Yes** button. When the closing entries appear, click on the **Post** button.

14. Display a post-closing trial balance.

    Click on the **Reports** toolbar button and click on **Ledger Reports**. Click on **Trial Balance** and the OK button to choose a report to display. To print the report, click on the **Print** button.

15. Click on the **Save As** toolbar button to save your data file. Key a file name of XXX6-3AP (where XXX are your initials, 6-3A represents the problem number, and P represents post closing). Click on the OK button.

Problem 6–3B
Sales-related and purchase-related transactions
Objective 2

The accounts and their balances in the ledger of The Document Company on April 1 of the current year are as follows:

Cash	$27,058
Accounts Receivable	12,000
Merchandise Inventory	82,142
Prepaid Insurance	3,200
Office Supplies	970
Accounts Payable	8,000
Roberta Stevens, Capital	99,660
Roberta Stevens, Drawing	12,000
Sales	75,850
Sales Returns & Allowances	5,000
Sales Discounts	700
Cost of Merchandise Sold	13,280
Sales Salaries Expense	10,000
Advertising Expense	5,500
Credit Card Expense	210
Miscellaneous Selling Expense	250
Office Salaries Expense	6,000
Rent Expense	5,000
Miscellaneous Administrative Expense	200

The following were selected from among the transactions completed by The Document Company during April of the current year:

Apr. 4. Purchased merchandise on account from Vela Co., list price $20,000, trade discount 40%, terms FOB destination, 2/10, n/30.
      5. Sold merchandise for cash, $4,100. The cost of the merchandise sold was $2,450.
      7. Purchased merchandise on account from Summit Co., $7,500, terms FOB shipping point, 2/10, n/30, with prepaid transportation costs of $200 added to the invoice.
      7. Returned $2,500 of merchandise purchased on April 4 from Vela Co.
     11. Sold merchandise on account to Bowles Co., list price $2,250, trade discount 20%, terms 1/10, n/30. The cost of the merchandise sold was $1,050.
     14. Paid Vela Co. on account for purchase of April 4, less return of April 7 and discount.
     15. Sold merchandise on nonbank credit cards and reported accounts to the card company, American Express, $5,850. The cost of the merchandise sold was $3,900.
     17. Paid Summit Co. on account for purchase of April 7, less discount.
     21. Received cash on account from sale of April 11 to Bowles Co., less discount.
     25. Sold merchandise on account to Clemons Co., $3,200, terms 1/10, n/30. The cost of the merchandise sold was $2,025.

Apr. 28. Received cash from American Express for nonbank credit card sales of April 15, less $280 service fee.
   30. Received merchandise returned by Clemons Co. from sale on April 25, $1,700. The cost of the returned merchandise was $810.

Instructions

Journalize the transactions.

DOS Instructions

1. Load the General Ledger Software program (IA1) from the program disk.

   Key **IA1** and press Enter at the DOS prompt. To the question "Read About General Ledger Software?" select **No** to bypass the copyright screens.

2. Load the file **06-3B** from the program disk.

   Press the **Alt** key to activate menu selection. Choose the **Open Accounting File** command in the File menu. Select the **Files** button and choose the accounting file to open. Select the Ok button to open the file.

3. Carefully key your name in the Student Name field in the General Information window. Press Ctrl+Enter to select Ok.

4. Choose the **Save As** command in the File menu and save the file to the drive and directory containing your data files. Key a file name of XXX6-3B (where XXX are your initials). Press Ctrl+Enter to select Ok.

5. Key the journal entries in the General Journal.

   Key the date for each transaction. Leave the Reference field blank. To display a list of accounts, press the F1 key. To display lists of vendors or customers, press the F2 and F3 keys, respectively. After each journal entry is keyed, press Ctrl+Enter to select Ok. When the Posting Summary window appears, press Ctrl+Enter to Post.

6. Display the journal entries.

   Select **Journals** from the Reports menu and select **General Journal** in the Report Selection window. Select the Ok button in the Selection Options window to display the journal entries for April. Press the F9 key to print the general journal report.

7. Make corrections to the journal entries, if necessary.

   Select **List** in the General Journal window to display the journal entries. Select the entry for correction and make the necessary change(s).

8. Display a trial balance.

   Select **Ledgers** from the Reports menu and select **Trial Balance** in the Report Selection window. Press the F9 key to print the trial balance report.

9. Key the adjusting entries in the General Journal based on the following data:

Insurance expired on April 30	$400.00
Office supplies on hand on April 30	$300.00

   Type the current year and enter 04/30 as the date for each entry. Key Adj.Ent. in the Reference field. To display a list of accounts, press the F1 key. After each entry is keyed, press Ctrl+Enter to select Ok. When the Posting Summary window appears, press Ctrl+Enter to Post.

10. Display the adjusting entries.

   Select **Journals** from the Reports menu and select **General Journal** in the Report Selection window. Key **Adj.Ent.** in the Reference restriction field of the Selection Options window. Press the Ok button to display the adjusting entries. Press the F9 key to print the general journal report.

11. Make corrections to the adjusting entries, if necessary.

   Select **List** in the General Journal window to display the adjusting entries. Select the entry for correction and make the necessary change(s).

12. Display the income statement, balance sheet, and statement of owner's equity.

    Select **Financial Statements** from the Reports menu and select **Income Statement, Balance Sheet,** and **Statement of Owner's Equity** in the Report Selection window. Press the F9 key to print each report.

13. Choose the **Save Accounting File** command in the File menu.

14. Perform period-end closing.

    Choose **Period-End Closing** from the Options menu. When the dialog box appears, press Ctrl+Enter to select Ok.

15. Display a post-closing trial balance.

    Select **Ledgers** from the Reports menu and select **Trial Balance** in the Report Selection window. Press the F9 key to print the trial balance report.

16. Choose the **Save As** command in the File menu to save your data file. Key a file name of XXX6-3BP (where XXX are your initials, 6-3B represents the problem number, and P represents post closing). Press Ctrl+Enter to select Ok.

Windows Instructions　　　　　　**To access Help, click on the Help button that appears in most windows.**

1. Click on the **Open** toolbar button and double-click on 06-3B to open the file.

2. Carefully key your name in the User Name field and click on the OK button.

3. Click on the **Save As** toolbar button and save the file to the drive and directory containing your data files. Key a file name of XXX6-3B (where XXX are your initials). Click on the OK button.

4. Click on the **Journal** toolbar button and key the journal entries in the General Journal.

    Key the date for each transaction. Leave the Reference field blank. When appropriate, key the vendor/customer name (or select the vendor/customer name from the drop-down list). After each journal entry is keyed, click on the **Post** button (or press Enter).

5. Display the journal entries.

    Click on the **Reports** toolbar button and click on **Journals** in the Report Selection window. Click on **General Journal** and the OK button to choose a report to display. Click on **Include All Journal Entries** and the OK button to display the general journal report. To print the report, click on the **Print** button.

6. Make corrections to the journal entries, if necessary.

    In the General Journal window, click on the entry to correct, then key the correction(s) to the journal entry and click on the **Post** button (or press Enter).

7. Display a trial balance.

    Click on the **Reports** toolbar button and click on **Ledger Reports**. Click on **Trial Balance** and the OK button to choose a report to display. To print the report, click on the **Print** button.

8. Key the adjusting entries in the General Journal based on the following data:

Insurance expired on April 30	$400.00
Office supplies on hand on April 30	$300.00

    Key 04/30/-- (where -- is the current year) for each entry. Key **Adj.Ent.** in the Reference field. After each entry is keyed, click on the **Post** button (or press Enter).

9. Display the adjusting entries.

    Click on the **Reports** toolbar button and click on **Journals** in the Report Selection window. Click on **General Journal** and the OK button to choose a report to display. Click on **Customize Journal Report** and select **Adj.Ent.** in the Reference drop-down list. Click on the OK button to display the adjusting entries report. To print the report, click on the **Print** button.

10. Make corrections to the adjusting entries, if necessary.

In the General Journal window, click on the entry to correct, then key the correction(s) to the journal entry and click on the **Post** button (or press Enter).

11. Display the income statement, balance sheet, and statement of owner's equity.

    Click on the **Reports** toolbar button and click on **Financial Statements**. Click on **Income Statement, Balance Sheet,** and **Statement of Owner's Equity.** To print each report, click on the **Print** button.

12. Click on the **Save** toolbar button to save your file.

13. Click on **Generate Closing Journal Entries** in the Options menu. When the dialog box appears, click on the **Yes** button. When the closing entries appear, click on the **Post** button.

14. Display a post-closing trial balance.

    Click on the **Reports** toolbar button and click on **Ledger Reports**. Click on **Trial Balance** and the OK button to choose a report to display. To print the report, click on the **Print** button.

15. Click on the **Save As** toolbar button to save your data file. Key a file name of XXX6-3BP (where XXX are your initials, 6-3B represents the problem number, and P represents post closing). Click on the OK button.

Comprehensive Problem 2

The Cycle Co. is a merchandising business. The account balances for The Cycle Co. as of May 1, 2000 (unless otherwise indicated) are as follows:

110	Cash	$ 29,160
111	Notes Receivable	—
112	Accounts Receivable	56,220
113	Interest Receivable	—
115	Merchandise Inventory	123,900
116	Prepaid Insurance	3,750
117	Store Supplies	2,550
123	Store Equipment	54,300
124	Accumulated Depreciation—Store Equipment	12,600
210	Accounts Payable	38,500
211	Salaries Payable	—
310	F. R. Schwinn, Capital, June 1, 1999	179,270
311	F. R. Schwinn, Drawing	25,000
312	Income Summary	—
410	Sales	731,600
411	Sales Returns and Allowances	13,600
412	Sales Discounts	5,200
510	Cost of Merchandise Sold	497,540
520	Sales Salaries Expense	74,400
521	Advertising Expense	18,000
522	Depreciation Expense	—
523	Store Supplies Expense	—
529	Miscellaneous Selling Expense	2,800
530	Office Salaries Expense	29,400
531	Rent Expense	24,500
532	Insurance Expense	—
539	Miscellaneous Administrative Expense	1,650
611	Interest Revenue	—

During May, the last month of the fiscal year, the following transactions were completed:

May   1. Paid rent for May, $2,400.
       1. Received a $7,500 note receivable from Holmes Co. on account.
       2. Purchased merchandise on account from Lindsey Co., terms 2/10, n/30, FOB shipping point, $25,000.
       3. Paid transportation charges on purchase of May 2, $750.
       5. Sold merchandise on account to Richards Co., terms 2/10, n/30, FOB shipping point, $8,500. The cost of the merchandise sold was $5,000.
       7. Received $16,900 cash from Vasquez Co. on account, no discount.

May   10. Sold merchandise for cash, $18,300. The cost of the merchandise sold was $11,000.
       12. Paid for merchandise purchased on May 2, less discount.
       13. Received merchandise returned on sale of May 5, $1,500. The cost of the merchandise returned was $900.
       14. Paid advertising expense for last half of May, $2,500.
       15. Received cash from sale of May 5, less return of May 13 and discount.
       19. Purchased merchandise for cash, $7,400.
       19. Paid $25,950 to Chang Co. on account, no discount
       20. Sold merchandise on account to Petroski Co., terms 1/10, n/30, FOB shipping point, $16,000. The cost of the merchandise sold was $9,600.
       21. For the convenience of the customer, paid shipping charges on sale of May 20, $600.
       21. Received $31,000 cash from Sinnett Co. on account, no discount.
       21. Purchased merchandise on account from Hummer Co., terms 1/10, n/30, FOB destination, $15,000.
       24. Returned $2,500 of damaged merchandise purchased on May 21, receiving credit from the seller.
       25. Refunded cash on sales made for cash, $750. The cost of the merchandise returned was $480.
       27. Paid sales salaries of $2,700 and office salaries of $900.
       29. Purchased store supplies for cash, $350.
       30. Sold merchandise on account to Brown Co., terms 2/10, n/30, FOB shipping point, $43,100. The cost of the merchandise sold was $25,000.
       30. Received cash from sale of May 20, less discount, plus transportation paid on May 21.
       31. Paid for purchase of May 21, less return of May 24 and discount.

Instructions

(*Note:* If the work sheet described in the appendix is used, follow the alternative instructions.)

1. Enter the balances of each of the accounts in the appropriate balance column of a four-column account. Write *Balance* in the item section, and place a check mark (✓) in the Posting Reference column.
2. Journalize the transactions for May.
3. Post the journal to the general ledger, extending the month-end balances to the appropriate balance columns after all posting is completed. In this problem, you are not required to update or post to the accounts receivable and accounts payable subsidiary ledgers.
4. Journalize and post the adjusting entries, using the following adjustment data:

a. Interest accrued on notes receivable on May 31		$ 100
b. Merchandise inventory on May 31		110,000
c. Insurance expired during the year		1,250
d. Store supplies on hand on May 31		1,050
e. Depreciation for the current year		8,860
f. Accrued salaries on May 31:		
Sales salaries	$400	
Office salaries	140	540

5. Prepare a multiple-step income statement, a statement of owner's equity, and a report form of balance sheet.
6. Journalize and post the closing entries. Indicate closed accounts by inserting a line in both balance columns opposite the closing entry. Insert the new balance in the owner's capital account.
7. Prepare a post-closing trial balance.

Alternative Instructions

1. Enter the balances of each of the accounts in the appropriate balance column of a four-column account. Write *Balance* in the item section, and place a check mark (✓) in the Posting Reference column.
2. Journalize the transactions for May.
3. Post the journal to the general ledger, extending the month-end balances to the appropriate balance columns after all posting is completed. In this problem, you are not required to update or post to the accounts receivable and accounts payable subsidiary ledgers.

4. Prepare a trial balance as of May 31 on a ten-column work sheet, listing all accounts in the order given in the ledger. Complete the work sheet for the fiscal year ended May 31, using the following adjustment data:

a. Interest accrued on notes receivable on May 31 $ 100
b. Merchandise inventory on May 31   110,000
c. Insurance expired during the year   1,250
d. Store supplies on hand on May 31   1,050
e. Depreciation for the current year   8,860
f. Accrued salaries on May 31:
     Sales salaries $400
     Office salaries   <u>140</u>   540

5. Prepare a multiple-step income statement, a statement of owner's equity, and a report form of balance sheet.

6. Journalize and post the adjusting entries.

7. Journalize and post the closing entries. Indicate closed accounts by inserting a line in both balance columns opposite the closing entry. Insert the new balance in the owner's capital account.

8. Prepare a post-closing trial balance.

DOS Instructions

1. Load the General Ledger Software program (IA1) from the program disk.

   Key **IA1** and press Enter at the DOS prompt. To the question "Read About General Ledger Software?" select **No** to bypass the copyright screens.

2. Load the file **C-2** from the program disk.

   Press the **Alt** key to activate menu selection. Choose the **Open Accounting File** command in the File menu. Select the **Files** button and choose the accounting file to open. Select the Ok button to open the file.

3. Carefully key your name in the Student Name field in the General Information window. Press Ctrl+Enter to select Ok.

4. Choose the **Save As** command in the File menu and save the file to the drive and directory containing your data files. Key a file name of XXXC-2 (where XXX are your initials). Press Ctrl+Enter to select Ok.

5. Key the journal entries in the General Journal.

   Type 2000 as the current year and enter the date for each transaction. Leave the Reference field blank. To display a list of accounts, press the F1 key. To display lists of vendors or customers, press the F2 and F3 keys, respectively. After each journal entry is keyed, press Ctrl+Enter to select Ok. When the Posting Summary window appears, press Ctrl+Enter to Post.

6. Display the journal entries.

   Select **Journals** from the Reports menu and select **General Journal** in the Report Selection window. Select the Ok button in the Selection Options window to display the journal entries for May. Press the F9 key to print the general journal report.

7. Make corrections to the journal entries, if necessary.

   Select **List** in the General Journal window to display the journal entries. Select the entry for correction and make the necessary change(s).

8. Display a trial balance.

   Select **Ledgers** from the Reports menu and select **Trial Balance** in the Report Selection window. Press the F9 key to print the trial balance report.

9. Key the adjusting entries in the General Journal.

   Type 2000 as the current year and enter 05/31 as the date for each entry. Key Adj.Ent. in the Reference field. To display a list of accounts, press the F1 key. After each entry is keyed, press Ctrl+Enter to select Ok. When the Posting Summary window appears, press Ctrl+Enter to Post.

10. Display the adjusting entries.

Select **Journals** from the Reports menu and select **General Journal** in the Report Selection window. Key **Adj.Ent.** in the Reference restriction field of the Selection Options window. Press the Ok button to display the adjusting entries. Press the F9 key to print the general journal report.

11. Make corrections to the adjusting entries, if necessary.

Select **List** in the General Journal window to display the adjusting entries. Select the entry for correction and make the necessary change(s).

12. Display the income statement, balance sheet, and statement of owner's equity.

Select **Financial Statements** from the Reports menu and select **Income Statement, Balance Sheet,** and **Statement of Owner's Equity** in the Report Selection window. Press the F9 key to print each report.

13. Choose the **Save Accounting File** command in the File menu.

14. Perform period-end closing.

Choose **Period-End Closing** from the Options menu. When the dialog box appears, press Ctrl+Enter to select Ok.

15. Display a post-closing trial balance.

Select **Ledgers** from the Reports menu and select **Trial Balance** in the Report Selection window. Press the F9 key to print the trial balance report.

16. Choose the **Save As** command in the File menu to save your data file. Key a file name of XXXC-2P (where XXX are your initials, C-2 represents the problem number, and P represents post closing). Press Ctrl+Enter to select Ok.

Windows Instructions　　　**To access Help, click on the Help button that appears in most windows.**

1. Click on the **Open** toolbar button and double-click on C-2 to open the file.

2. Carefully key your name in the User Name field and click on the OK button.

3. Click on the **Save As** toolbar button and save the file to the drive and directory containing your data files. Key a file name of XXXC-2 (where XXX are your initials). Click on the OK button.

4. Click on the **Journal** toolbar button and key the journal entries in the General Journal.

Key the date for each transaction. Leave the Reference field blank. When appropriate, key the vendor/customer name (or select the vendor/customer name from the drop-down list). After each journal enry is keyed, click on the **Post** button (or press Enter).

5. Display the journal entries.

Click on the **Reports** toolbar button and click on **Journals** in the Report Selection window. Click on **General Journal** and the OK button to choose a report to display. Click on **Include All Journal Entries** and the OK button to display the general journal report. To print the report, click on the **Print** button.

6. Make corrections to the journal entries, if necessary.

In the General Journal window, click on the entry to correct, then key the correction(s) to the journal entry and click on the **Post** button (or press Enter).

7. Display a trial balance.

Click on the **Reports** toolbar button and click on **Ledger Reports**. Click on **Trial Balance** and the OK button to choose a report to display. To print the report, click on the **Print** button.

8. Key the adjusting entries in the General Journal.

Key 05/31/00 as the date for each entry. Key **Adj.Ent.** in the Reference field. After each entry is keyed, click on the **Post** button (or press Enter).

9. Display the adjusting entries.

Click on the **Reports** toolbar button and click on **Journals** in the Report Selection window. Click on **General Journal** and the OK button to choose a report to display. Click on **Customize**

Journal Report and select **Adj.Ent.** in the Reference drop-down list. Click on the OK button to display the adjusting entries report. To print the report, click on the **Print** button.

10. Make corrections to the adjusting entries, if necessary.

In the General Journal window, click on the entry to correct, then key the correction(s) to the journal entry and click on the **Post** button (or press Enter).

11. Display the income statement, balance sheet, and statement of owner's equity.

Click on the **Reports** toolbar button and click on **Financial Statements**. Click on **Income Statement, Balance Sheet,** and **Statement of Owner's Equity.** To print each report, click on the **Print** button.

12. Click on the **Save** toolbar button to save your file.

13. Click on **Generate Closing Journal Entries** in the Options menu. When the dialog box appears, click on the **Yes** button. When the closing entries appear, click on the **Post** button.

14. Display a post-closing trial balance.

Click on the **Reports** toolbar button and click on **Ledger Reports**. Click on **Trial Balance** and the OK button to choose a report to display. To print the report, click on the **Print** button.

15. Click on the **Save As** toolbar button to save your data file. Key a file name of XXXC-2P (where XXX are your initials, C-2 represents the problem number, and P represents post closing). Click on the OK button.

Problem 8–5A
Sales and notes receivable transactions
Objective 7

The accounts and their balances in the ledger of Wurtz Co. on January 10 of the current year are as follows:

Cash..	$38,337
Accounts Receivable..	9,500
Merchandise Inventory..	64,000
Accounts Payable	35,000
Steven Wurtz, Capital	173,787
Steven Wurtz, Drawing	30,000
Sales	37,000
Cost of Merchandise Sold	26,000
Sales Salaries Expense	40,500
Advertising Expense	8,000
Miscellaneous Selling Expense.......................................	500
Office Salaries Expense..	16,500
Rent Expense..	12,250
Miscellaneous Administrative Expense............................	200

The following were selected from among the transactions completed by Wurtz Co. during the current year. Wurtz Co. sells and installs home and business security systems.

Jan. 10. Loaned $25,000 cash to Joyce Yang, receiving a 90-day, 8% note.
Feb. 1. Sold merchandise on account to Spencer and Son, $12,000. The cost of the merchandise sold was $8,800.
      10. Sold merchandise on account to Roper Co., $40,000. The cost of merchandise sold was $30,000.
Mar. 3. Accepted a 60-day, 10% note for $12,000 from Spencer and Son on account.
      11. Accepted a 60-day, 12% note for $40,000 from Roper Co. on account.
Apr. 10. Received the interest due from Joyce Yang and a new 90-day, 12% note as a renewal of the loan of January 10. (Record both the debit and the credit to the notes receivable account.)
May   2. Received from Spencer and Son the amount due on the note of March 3.
      10. Roper Co. dishonored its note dated March 11.
June 9. Received from Roper Co. the amount owed on the dishonored note, plus interest for 30 days at 15% computed on the maturity value of the note.
July 9. Received from Joyce Yang the amount due on her note of April 10.
Aug. 23. Sold merchandise on account to C. D. Connors Co., $8,000. The cost of the merchandise sold was $5,000.

Sep.   2. Received from C. D. Connors Co. the amount of the invoice of August 23, less 1% discount.

Instructions

Journalize the transactions.

DOS Instructions

1. Load the General Ledger Software program (IA1).

2. Load the file **08-5A** from the program disk.

3. Carefully key your name in the Student Name field.

4. Save the file with a file name of XXX8-5A (where XXX are your initials).

5. Key the journal entries in the General Journal. Key the customer number in the Ven./Cus. field when the transaction involves Accounts Receivable. Press the F3 key to display a customer list.

6. Display the journal entries. Key a date range of 01/01/-- to 12/31/-- (where -- is the current year).

7. Make corrections to the journal entries, if necessary.

8. Display the income statement, balance sheet, and statement of owner's equity.

9. Save your data file.

Windows Instructions

To access Help, click on the Help button that appears in most windows.

1. Open the file **08-5A**.

2. Carefully key your name in the User Name field.

3. Save the file with a file name of XXX8-5A (where XXX are your initials).

4. Key the journal entries in the General Journal. Click on the customer name in the drop-down list when the transaction involves Accounts Receivable.

5. Display the journal entries.

6. Make corrections to the journal entries, if necessary.

7. Display the income statement, balance sheet, and statement of owner's equity.

8. Save your data file.

Problem 8–5B
Sales and notes receivable transactions
Objective 7

The accounts and their balances in the ledger of Cady Co. on January 10 of the current year are as follows:

Cash	$48,329
Accounts Receivable	9,500
Merchandise Inventory	28,000
Accounts Payable	10,000
Maria Cady, Capital	175,779
Maria Cady, Drawing	31,000
Sales	74,525
Cost of Merchandise Sold	37,000
Sales Salaries Expense	45,500
Advertising Expense	7,500
Miscellaneous Selling Expense	1,250
Office Salaries Expense	26,500
Rent Expense	25,500
Miscellaneous Administrative Expense	225

The following were selected from among the transactions completed during the current year by Cady Co., an appliance wholesale company:

Jan.　11. Sold merchandise on account to Hayden Co., $18,000. The cost of merchandise sold was $12,000.

Mar.　3. Accepted a 60-day, 10% note for $18,000 from Hayden Co. on account.

May　2. Received from Hayden Co. the amount due on the note of March 13.

June　1. Sold merchandise on account to Kohl's for $5,000. The cost of merchandise sold was $3,500.

　　　5. Loaned $9,000 cash to Frank Scharf, receiving a 30-day, 12% note.

　　11. Received from Kohl's the amount due on the invoice of June 1, less 2% discount.

July　5. Received the interest due from Frank Scharf and a new 60-day, 14% note as a renewal of the loan of June 5. (Record both the debit and the credit to the notes receivable account.)

Sept.　3. Received from Frank Scharf the amount due on his note of July 5.

　　　4. Sold merchandise on account to Nugent Co., $5,000. The cost of merchandise sold was $3,500.

Oct.　4. Accepted a 60-day, 12% note for $5,000 from Nugent Co. on account.

Dec.　3. Nugent Co. dishonored the note dated October 4.

　　23. Received from Nugent Co. the amount owed on the dishonored note, plus interest for 20 days at 12% computed on the maturity value of the note.

Instructions

Journalize the transactions.

DOS Instructions

1. Load the General Ledger Software program (IA1).

2. Load the file **08-5B** from the program disk.

3. Carefully key your name in the Student Name field.

4. Save the file with a file name of XXX8-5B (where XXX are your initials).

5. Key the journal entries in the General Journal. Key the customer number in the Ven./Cus. field when the transaction involves Accounts Receivable. Press the F3 key to display a customer list.

6. Display the journal entries. Key a date range of 01/01/-- to 12/31/-- (where -- is the current year).

7. Make corrections to the journal entries, if necessary.

8. Display the income statement, balance sheet, and statement of owner's equity.

9. Save your data file.

Windows Instructions

1. Load the General Ledger Software program (IA1).

2. Load the file **08-5B** from the program disk.

3. Carefully key your name in the Student Name field.

4. Save the file with a file name of XXX8-5B (where XXX are your initials).

5. Key the journal entries in the General Journal. Click on the customer name in the drop-down list when the transaction involves Accounts Receivable.

6. Display the journal entries.

7. Make corrections to the journal entries, if necessary.

8. Display the income statement, balance sheet, and statement of owner's equity.

9. Save your data file.

Problem 11–1A
Liability transactions
Objectives 2, 3

The accounts and their balances in the ledger of Renaissance Products Co. on January 1 of the current year are as follows:

110	Cash	$ 112,760
120	Accounts Receivable	53,340
130	Merchandise Inventory..	121,400
141	Prepaid Insurance...	2,480

142	Supplies	2,120
151	Office Equipment	115,900
152	Accumulated Depreciation—Office Equipment	66,600
153	Tools	50,300
154	Accumulated Depreciation—Tools	18,000
210	Accounts Payable	32,000
310	Maurice Blalock, Capital	103,504
320	Maurice Blalock, Drawing	80,000
410	Sales	1,045,500
510	Cost of Merchandise Sold	513,375
610	Sales Salaries Expense	82,800
611	Advertising Expense	23,300
619	Miscellaneous Selling Expense	1,600
710	Office Salaries Expense	52,200
711	Rent Expense	25,000
712	Heating & Lighting Expense	17,400
713	Taxes Expense	7,850
719	Miscellaneous Administrative Expense	3,500
910	Interest Expense	279

The following items were selected from among the transactions completed by Renaissance Products Co. during the current year:

Feb. 15. Purchased merchandise on account from Ranier Co., $14,000, terms n/30.

Mar. 17. Issued a 30-day, 9% note for $14,000 to Ranier Co., on account.

Apr. 16. Paid Ranier Co. the amount owed on the note of March 17.

July 15. Borrowed $20,000 from Security Bank, issuing a 90-day, 12% note.

25. Purchased tools by issuing a $60,000, 120-day note to Sun Supply Co., which discounted the note at the rate of 13%.

Oct. 13. Paid Security Bank the interest due on the note of July 15 and renewed the loan by issuing a new 30-day, 15% note for $20,000. (Journalize both the debit and credit to the notes payable account.)

Nov. 12. Paid Security Bank the amount due on the note of October 13.

22. Paid Sun Supply Co. the amount due on the note of July 25.

Dec. 1. Purchased office equipment from Valley Equipment Co. for $75,000, paying $15,000 and issuing a series of ten 12% notes for $6,000 each, coming due at 30-day intervals.

17. Settled a product liability lawsuit with a customer for $35,000, payable in January. Renaissance accrued the loss in a litigation claim payable account

31. Paid the amount due Valley Equipment Co. on the first note in the series issued on December 1.

Instructions

1. Journalize the transactions.
2. Journalize the adjusting entry for each of the following accrued expenses at the end of the current year: (a) product warranty cost, $15,450; (b) interest on the nine notes owed to Valley Equipment Co.

DOS Instructions

1. Load the General Ledger Software program (IA1).

2. Load the file **11-1A** from the program disk.

3. Carefully key your name in the Student Name field.

4. Save the file with a file name of XXX11-1A (where XXX are your initials).

5. Key the journal entries in the General Journal. Key the vendor number in the Ven./Cus. field when the transaction involves Accounts Payable. Press the F2 key to display a vendor list.

6. Display the journal entries. Key a date range of 01/01/-- to 12/31/-- (where -- is the current year).

7. Make corrections to the journal entries, if necessary.

8. Display a trial balance.

9. Key the adjusting entries in the General Journal. Key **Adj.Ent.** in the Reference field.

10. Display the adjusting entries. Key **Adj.Ent.** in the Reference restriction field to display only the adjusting entries.

11. Display the income statement, balance sheet, and statement of owner's equity.

12. Use the **Save Accounting File** command to save your data file.

13. Perform period-end closing.

14. Display a post-closing trial balance.

15. Use the **Save As** command and save your data file with a file name of XXX111AP (where XXX are your initials, 111A represents the problem number, and P represents post closing).

Windows Instructions

To access Help, click on the Help button that appears in most windows.

1. Open the file **11-1A**.

2. Carefully key your name in the User Name field.

3. Save the file with a file name of XXX11-1A (where XXX are your initials).

4. Key the journal entries in the General Journal. Click on the vendor name in the drop-down list when the transaction involves Accounts Payable.

5. Display the journal entries.

6. Make corrections to the journal entries, if necessary.

7. Display a trial balance.

8. Key the adjusting entries in the General Journal. Key **Adj.Ent.** in the Reference field.

9. Display the adjusting entries. Click on **Adj.Ent.** in the Reference drop-down list to display only the adjusting entries.

10. Display the income statement, balance sheet, and statement of owner's equity.

11. Click on the **Save** toolbar button to save your data file.

12. Generate and post the closing journal entries.

13. Display a post-closing trial balance.

14. Click on the **Save As** toolbar button to save your data file. Key a file name of XXX111AP (where XXX are your initials, 111A represents the problem number, and P represents post closing).

Problem 11–6A
Payroll accounts and
year-end entries
Objectives 4, 5, 6

The following accounts, with the balances indicated, appear in the ledger of Mid States CableView Co. on December 1 of the current year:

110	Cash	$ 239,901
120	Accounts Receivable	188,203
130	Merchandise Inventory	281,627
141	Prepaid Insurance	4,050
142	Store Supplies	7,825
151	Store Equipment	162,300
152	Accumulated Depreciation—Store Equipment	44,980
210	Accounts Payable	78,061
212	Social Security Tax Payable	7,784
213	Medicare Tax Payable	2,048
214	Employees' Federal Income Tax Payable	12,632
215	Employees' State Income Tax Payable	12,291
216	State Unemployment Tax Payable	1,240
217	Federal Unemployment Tax Payable	325
218	Bond Deductions Payable	1,400

219	Medical Insurance Payable	4,500
310	Daniel West, Capital	609,829
320	Daniel West, Drawing	150,000
410	Sales	3,771,200
510	Cost of Merchandise Sold	1,646,000
611	Operations Salaries Expense	915,200
612	Advertising Expense	47,100
613	Depreciation Expense—Store Equipment	13,041
614	Store Supplies Expense	36,926
615	Miscellaneous Selling Expense	9,050
711	Officers Salaries Expense	365,300
712	Office Salaries Expense	221,700
713	Rent Expense	74,500
714	Heating & Lighting Expense	29,650
715	Insurance Expense	27,551
716	Miscellaneous Administrative Expense	6,800
719	Payroll Taxes Expense	119,566

The following transactions relating to payroll, payroll deductions, and payroll taxes occurred during December:

Dec. 2. Issued Check No. 728 for $1,400 to First National Bank to purchase U.S. savings bonds for employees.

3. Issued Check No. 729 to First National Bank for $22,464, in payment of $7,784 of social security tax, $2,048 of Medicare tax, and $12,632 of employees' federal income tax due.

14. Journalized the entry to record the biweekly payroll. A summary of the payroll record follows:

Salary distribution:

Operations	$42,400	
Officers	16,220	
Office	10,450	$69,070

Deductions:

Social security tax	$ 3,799	
Medicare tax	1,036	
Federal income tax withheld	12,294	
State income tax withheld	3,108	
Savings bond deductions	700	
Medical insurance deductions	750	21,687
Net amount		$47,383

14. Issued Check No. 738 in payment of the net amount of the biweekly payroll.

14. Journalized the entry to record payroll taxes on employees' earnings of December 14: social security tax, $3,799; Medicare tax, $1,036; state unemployment tax, $286; federal unemployment tax, $77.

17. Issued Check No. 744 to First National Bank for $21,964, in payment of $7,598 of social security tax, $2,072 of Medicare tax, and $12,294 of employees' federal income tax due.

18. Issued Check No. 750 to Pico Insurance Company for $4,500, in payment of the semiannual premium on the group medical insurance policy.

28. Journalized the entry to record the biweekly payroll. A summary of the payroll record follows:

Salary distribution:

Operations	$40,800	
Officers	16,350	
Office	10,580	$67,730

Deductions:

Social security tax	$ 3,657	
Medicare tax	1,016	
Federal income tax withheld	12,056	
State income tax withheld	3,048	
Savings bond deduction	700	20,477
Net amount		$47,253

Dec. 28. Issued Check No. 782 in payment of the net amount of the biweekly payroll.

28. Journalized the entry to record payroll taxes on employees' earnings of December 28: social security tax, $3,657; Medicare tax, $1,016; state unemployment tax, $174; federal unemployment tax, $38.

30. Issued Check No. 791 to First National Bank for $1,400 to purchase U.S. savings bonds for employees.

30. Issued Check No. 792 for $18,447 to First National Bank in payment of employees' state income tax due on December 31.

31. Paid $46,000 of the annual pension cost of $50,000. (Record both the payment and un-funded pension liability.)

Instructions

1. Journalize the transactions.
2. Journalize the following adjusting entries on December 31:
   a. Salaries accrued: operations salaries, $4,080; officers salaries, $1,635; office salaries, $1,058. The payroll taxes are immaterial and are not accrued.
   b. Vacation pay, $12,500.

DOS Instructions

1. Load the General Ledger Software program (IA1).

2. Load the file **11-6A** from the program disk.

3. Carefully key your name in the Student Name field.

4. Save the file with a file name of XXX11-6A (where XXX are your initials).

5. Key the journal entries in the General Journal.

   Note: Because the journal entry parts are more than one screen can accommodate, the entries to record the biweekly payroll on December 14 and December 28 must be split between two data entry windows. Enter as many parts of the transaction as you can and post the entry. Answer "Yes" to the question, "Out of Balance. Proceed anyway?" Record the remainder of the transaction in the next data entry window.

6. Display the journal entries.

7. Make corrections to the journal entries, if necessary.

8. Display a trial balance.

9. Key the adjusting entries in the General Journal. Key **Adj.Ent.** in the Reference field.

10. Display the adjusting entries. Key **Adj.Ent.** in the Reference restriction field to display only the adjusting entries.

11. Display the income statement, balance sheet, and statement of owner's equity.

12. Use the **Save Accounting File** command to save your data file.

13. Perform period-end closing.

14. Display a post-closing trial balance.

15. Use the **Save As** command and save your data file with a file name of XXX116AP (where XXX are your initials, 116A represents the problem number, and P represents post closing).

Windows Instructions

To access Help, click on the Help button that appears in most windows.

1. Open the file **11-6A**.

2. Carefully key your name in the User Name field.

3. Save the file with a file name of XXX11-6A (where XXX are your initials).

4. Key the journal entries in the General Journal.

5. Display the journal entries.

6. Make corrections to the journal entries, if necessary.

7. Display a trial balance.

8. Key the adjusting entries in the General Journal. Key **Adj.Ent.** in the Reference field.

9. Display the adjusting entries. Click on **Adj.Ent.** in the Reference drop-down list to display only the adjusting entries.

10. Display the income statement, balance sheet, and statement of owner's equity.

11. Click on the **Save** toolbar buttonto save your data file.

12. Generate and post the closing journal entries.

13. Display a post-closing trial balance.

14. Click on the **Save As** toolbar button to save your data file. Key a file name of XXX116AP (where XXX are your initials, 116A represents the problem number, and P represents post closing).

Problem 11–1B
Liability transactions
Objectives 2, 3

The accounts and their balances in the ledger of Pride Polymers on January 1 of the current year are as follows:

110	Cash	$169,600
120	Accounts Receivable	52,120
130	Merchandise Inventory	119,670
141	Prepaid Insurance	2,530
142	Supplies	2,070
151	Equipment	53,300
152	Accumulated Depreciation—Equipment	33,200
153	Store Equipment	50,000
154	Accumulated Depreciation—Store Equipment	23,000
210	Accounts Payable	31,500
310	Alfred DiNiro, Capital	249,404
320	Alfred DiNiro, Drawing	57,202
410	Sales	899,761
510	Cost of Merchandise Sold	516,314
610	Sales Salaries Expense	81,760
611	Advertising Expense	22,980
619	Miscellaneous Selling Expense	1,400
710	Office Salaries Expense	51,678
711	Rent Expense	23,000
712	Heating & Lighting Expense	19,500
713	Taxes Expense	10,635
719	Miscellaneous Administrative Expense	2,800
910	Interest Expense	306

The following items were selected from among the transactions completed by Pride Polymers during the current year:

April 7. Borrowed $12,000 from First Financial Corporation, issuing a 60-day, 12% note for that amount.

May 10. Purchased equipment by issuing a $60,000, 120-day note to Milford Equipment Co., which discounted the note at the rate of 10%.

June 6. Paid First Financial Corporation the interest due on the note of April 7 and renewed the loan by issuing a new 30-day, 16% note for $12,000. (Record both the debit and credit to the notes payable account.)

July 6. Paid First Financial Corporation the amount due on the note of June 6.

Aug. 3. Purchased merchandise on account from Hamilton Co., $25,000, terms, n/30.

Sep. 2. Issued a 60-day, 15% note for $25,000 to Hamilton Co., on account.

7. Paid Milford Equipment Co. the amount due on the note of May 10.

Nov. 1. Paid Hamilton Co. the amount owed on the note of September 2.

15. Purchased store equipment from Shingo Equipment Co. for $80,000, paying $17,000 and issuing a series of seven 12% notes for $9,000 each, coming due at 30-day intervals.

Dec.   15. Paid the amount due Shingo Equipment Co. on the first note in the series issued on November 15.
        21. Settled a product liability lawsuit with a customer for $50,000, to be paid in January. Pride Polymers accrued the loss in a litigation claims payable account.

Instructions

1. Journalize the transactions.
2. Journalize the adjusting entry for each of the following accrued expenses at the end of the current year:
   a. Product warranty cost, $9,500.
   b. Interest on the six remaining notes owed to Shingo Equipment Co.

DOS Instructions

1. Load the General Ledger Software program (IA1).

2. Load the file **11-1B** from the program disk.

3. Carefully key your name in the Student Name field.

4. Save the file with a file name of XXX11-1B (where XXX are your initials).

5. Key the journal entries in the General Journal. Key the vendor number in the Ven./Cus. field when the transaction involves Accounts Payable. Press the F2 key to display a vendor list.

6. Display the journal entries. Key a date range of 04/01/-- to 12/31/-- (where -- is the current year).

7. Make corrections to the journal entries, if necessary.

8. Display a trial balance.

9. Key the adjusting entries in the General Journal. Key **Adj.Ent.** in the Reference field.

10. Display the adjusting entries. Key **Adj.Ent.** in the Reference restriction field to display only the adjusting entries.

11. Display the income statement, balance sheet, and statement of owner's equity.

12. Use the **Save Accounting File** command to save your data file.

13. Perform period-end closing.

14. Display a post-closing trial balance.

15. Use the **Save As** command and save your data file with a file name of XXX111BP (where XXX are your initials, 111B represents the problem number, and P represents post closing).

Windows Instructions

To access Help, click on the Help button that appears in most windows.

1. Open the file **11-1B**.

2. Carefully key your name in the User Name field.

3. Save the file with a file name of XXX11-1B where XXX are your initials).

4. Key the journal entries in the General Journal. Click on the vendor name in the drop-down list when the transaction involves Accounts Payable.

5. Display the journal entries.

6. Make corrections to the journal entries, if necessary.

7. Display a trial balance.

8. Key the adjusting entries in the General Journal. **Key Adj.Ent.** in the Reference field.

9. Display the adjusting entries. Click on **Adj.Ent.** in the Reference drop-down list to display only the adjusting entries.

10. Display the income statement, balance sheet, and statement of owner's equity.

11. Click on the **Save** toolbar button to save your data file.

12. Generate and post the closing journal entries.

13. Display a post-closing trial balance.

14. Click on the **Save As** toolbar button to save your data file. Key a file name of XXX111BP (where XXX are your initials, 111B represents the problem number, and P represents post closing).

Problem 11–6B
Payroll accounts and year-end entries
Objectives 4, 5, 6

The following accounts, with the balances indicated, appear in the ledger of Teton Outdoor Equipment Company on December 1 of the current year:

110	Cash	$ 334,690
120	Accounts Receivable	192,300
130	Merchandise Inventory	261,450
141	Prepaid Insurance	4,250
142	Store Supplies	7,980
151	Store Equipment	161,100
152	Accumulated Depreciation—Store Equipment	45,540
210	Accounts Payable	80,400
212	Social Security Tax Payable	6,232
213	Medicare Tax Payable	1,640
214	Employees' Federal Income Tax Payable	10,113
215	Employees' State Income Tax Payable	9,839
216	State Unemployment Tax Payable	1,104
217	Federal Unemployment Tax Payable	288
218	Bond Deductions Payable	1,050
219	Medical Insurance Payable	3,800
310	Peggy Ann Ibis, Capital	642,990
320	Peggy Ann Ibis, Drawing	110,000
410	Sales	3,387,200
510	Cost of Merchandise Sold	1,580,000
611	Sales Salaries Expense	784,600
612	Advertising Expense	47,400
613	Depreciation Expense—Store Equipment	13,662
614	Store Supplies Expense	35,850
615	Miscellaneous Selling Expense	8,250
711	Officers Salaries Expense	296,700
712	Office Salaries Expense	121,300
713	Rent Expense	72,000
714	Heating & Lighting Expense	28,980
715	Insurance Expense	26,921
716	Miscellaneous Administrative Expense	6,420
719	Payroll Taxes Expense	96,343

The following transactions relating to payroll, payroll deductions, and payroll taxes occurred during December:

Dec. 1. Issued Check No. 728 to Pico Insurance Company for $3,800, in payment of the semiannual premium on the group medical insurance policy.

2. Issued Check No. 729 to First National Bank for $17,985, in payment for $6,232 of social security tax, $1,640 of Medicare tax, and $10,113 of employees' federal income tax due.

3. Issued Check No. 730 for $1,050 to First National Bank to purchase U.S. savings bonds for employees.

14. Journalized the entry to record the biweekly payroll. A summary of the payroll record follows:

Salary distribution:

Sales	$36,110	
Officers	13,672	
Office	5,675	$55,457

Deductions:		
Social security tax	$ 3,050	
Medicare tax	832	
Federal income tax withheld	9,871	
State income tax withheld	2,496	
Savings bond deductions	525	
Medical insurance deductions	633	17,407
Net amount		$38,050

14. Issued Check No. 738 in payment of the net amount of the biweekly payroll.
14. Journalized the entry to record payroll taxes on employees' earnings of December 14: social security tax, $3,050; Medicare tax, $832; state unemployment tax, $242; federal unemployment tax, $65.
17. Issued Check No. 744 to First National Bank for $17,635, in payment for $6,100 of social security tax, $1,664 of Medicare tax, and $9,871 of employees' federal income tax due.
28. Journalized the entry to record the biweekly payroll. A summary of the payroll record follows:

Salary distribution:		
Sales	$37,450	
Officers	13,600	
Office	5,820	$56,870
Deductions:		
Social security tax	$ 3,071	
Medicare tax	853	
Federal income tax withheld	10,123	
State income tax withheld	2,559	
Savings bond deduction	525	17,131
Net amount		$39,739

28. Issued Check No. 782 for the net amount of the biweekly payroll.
28. Journalized the entry to record payroll taxes on employees' earnings of December 28: social security tax, $3,071; Medicare tax, $853; state unemployment tax, $196; federal unemployment tax, $44.
30. Issued Check No. 791 for $14,894 to First National Bank, in payment of employees' state income tax due on December 31.
30. Issued Check No. 792 to First National Bank for $1,050 to purchase U.S. savings bonds for employees.
31. Paid $57,700 of the annual pension cost of $65,000. (Record both the payment and the unfunded pension liability.)

Instructions

1. Journalize the transactions.
2. Journalize the following adjusting entries on December 31:
   a. Salaries accrued: sales salaries, $3,745; officers salaries, $1,360; office salaries, $582. The payroll taxes are immaterial and are not accrued.
   b. Vacation pay, $14,200.

DOS Instructions

1. Load the General Ledger Software program (IA1).

2. Load the file **11-6B** from the program disk.

3. Carefully key your name in the Student Name field.

4. Save the file with a file name of XXX11-6B (where XXX are your initials).

5. Key the journal entries in the General Journal.

   Note: Because the journal entry parts are more than one screen can accommodate, the entries to record the biweekly payroll on December 14 and December 28 must be split between two data entry windows. Enter as many parts of the transaction as you can and post the entry. Answer "Yes" to the question, "Out of Balance. Proceed anyway?" Record the remainder of the transaction in the next data entry window.

6. Display the journal entries.

7. Make corrections to the journal entries, if necessary.

8. Display a trial balance.

9. Key the adjusting entries in the General Journal. Key **Adj.Ent**. in the Reference field.

10. Display the adjusting entries. Key **Adj.Ent**. in the Reference restriction field to display only the adjusting entries.

11. Display the income statement, balance sheet, and statement of owner's equity.

12. Use the **Save Accounting File** command to save your data file.

13. Perform period-end closing.

14. Display a post-closing trial balance.

15. Use the **Save As** command and save your data file with a file name of XXX116BP (where XXX are your initials, 116B represents the problem number, and P represents post closing).

Windows Instructions   **To access Help, click on the Help button that appears in most windows.**

1. Open the file **11-6B**.

2. Carefully key your name in the User Name field.

3. Save the file with a file name of XXX11-6B (where XXX are your initials).

4. Key the journal entries in the General Journal.

5. Display the journal entries.

6. Make corrections to the journal entries, if necessary.

7. Display a trial balance.

8. Key the adjusting entries in the General Journal. Key **Adj.Ent**. in the Reference field.

9. Display the adjusting entries. Click on **Adj.Ent**. in the Reference drop-down list to display only the adjusting entries.

10. Display the income statement, balance sheet, and statement of owner's equity.

11. Click on the **Save** toolbar button to save your data file.

12. Generate and post the closing journal entries.

13. Display a post-closing trial balance.

14. Click on the **Save As** toolbar button to save your data file. Key a file name of XXX116BP (where XXX are your initials, 116B represents the problem number, and P represents post closing).

Comprehensive Problem 3

Selected transactions completed by Wacker Co. during its first fiscal year ending December 31 were as follows:

Jan.   2. Issued a check to establish a petty cash fund of $400.

Mar.   1. Replenished the petty cash fund, based on the following summary of petty cash receipts: office supplies, $144; miscellaneous selling expense, $97; miscellaneous administrative expense, $138.

Apr.   5. Purchased $8,000 of merchandise on account, terms 1/10, n/30. The perpetual inventory system is used to account for inventory.

May   5. Paid the invoice of April 5 after the discount period had passed.

     10. Received cash from daily cash sales for $8,710. The amount indicated by the cash register was $8,750.

June   2. Received a 60-day, 12% note for $40,000 on account.

Aug.   1. Received amount owed on June 2 note, plus interest at the maturity date.

Aug.   3. Received $700 on account and wrote off the remainder owed on a $1,000 accounts receivable balance. (The allowance method is used in accounting for uncollectible receivables.)

28. Reinstated the account written off on August 3 and received $300 cash in full payment.

Sep.   2. Purchased land by issuing a $30,000, 90-day note to Ace Development Co., which discounted it at 12%.

Oct.   1. Traded office equipment for new equipment with a list price of $140,000. A trade-in allowance of $25,000 was received on the old equipment that had cost $80,000 and had accumulated depreciation of $50,000 as of October 1. A 120-day, 12% note was issued for the balance owed.

Nov. 30. Journalized the monthly payroll for November, based on the following data:

Salaries:		Deductions:	
Sales salaries	$15,500	Income tax withheld	$3,885
Office salaries	5,500	Social security tax withheld	1,260
	$21,000	Medicare tax withheld	315

Unemployment tax rates:	
State unemployment	3.8%
Federal unemployment	0.8%
Amount subject to unemployment taxes:	
State unemployment	$500
Federal unemployment	500

30. Journalized the employer's payroll taxes on the payroll.

Dec.   1. Journalized the payment of the September 2 note at maturity.

30. The pension cost for the year was $40,000, of which $36,000 was paid to the pension plan trustee.

Instructions

1. Journalize the selected transactions.
2. Based on the following data, prepare a bank reconciliation for December of the current year:
   a. Balance according to the bank statement at December 31, $89,560.
   b. Balance according to the ledger at December 31, $69,685.
   c. Checks outstanding at December 31, $34,310.
   d. Deposit in transit, not recorded by bank, $14,200.
   e. Bank debit memorandum for service charges, $55.
   f. A check for $200 in payment of an invoice was incorrectly recorded in the accounts as $20.
3. Based on the bank reconciliation prepared in (2), journalize the entry or entries to be made by Wacker Co.
4. Based on the following selected data, journalize the adjusting entries as of December 31 of the current year:
   a. Estimated uncollectible accounts at December 31, $4,220. The balance of Allowance for Doubtful Accounts at December 31 was $800 (debit).
   b. The physical inventory on December 31 indicated an inventory shrinkage of $2,600.
   c. Prepaid insurance expired during the year, $14,400.
   d. Office supplies used during the year, $3,900.
   e. Depreciation is computed as follows:

Asset	Cost	Residual Value	Acquisition Date	Useful Life in Years	Depreciation Method Used
Buildings	$290,000	$ 0	January 2	50	Straight-line
Office Equip.	140,000	12,000	July 1	5	Straight-line
Store Equip.	90,000	10,000	January 3	8	Declining-balance (at twice the straight-line rate)

   f. A patent costing $36,000 when acquired on January 2 has a remaining legal life of 9 years and is expected to have value for 6 years.
   g. The cost of mineral rights was $80,000. Of the estimated deposit of 25,000 tons of ore, 4,000 tons were mined during the year.
   h. Total vacation pay expense for the year, $6,000.
   i. A product warranty was granted beginning December 1 and covering a one-year period. The estimated cost is 3% of sales, which totaled $390,000 in December.

5. Based on the following post-closing trial balance and other data, prepare a balance sheet in report form at December 31 of the current year.

Wacker Co.
Post-Closing Trial Balance
December 31, 2000

Petty Cash	400	
Cash	69,450	
Notes Receivable	50,000	
Accounts Receivable	194,300	
Allowance for Doubtful Accounts		4,220
Merchandise Inventory	40,250	
Prepaid Insurance	28,800	
Office Supplies	6,300	
Land	50,000	
Buildings	290,000	
Accumulated Depreciation—Buildings		5,800
Office Equipment	140,000	
Accumulated Depreciation—Office Equipment		12,800
Store Equipment	90,000	
Accumulated Depreciation—Store Equipment		22,500
Mineral Rights	80,000	
Accumulated Depletion		12,800
Patents	30,000	
Social Security Tax Payable		2,640
Medicare Tax Payable		660
Employees Federal Income Tax Payable		4,100
State Unemployment Tax Payable		45
Federal Unemployment Tax Payable		20
Salaries Payable		16,000
Accounts Payable		94,000
Product Warranty Payable		11,700
Vacation Pay Payable		6,000
Unfunded Pension Liability		4,000
Notes Payable		450,000
B. Wacker, Capital		422,215
	1,069,500	1,069,500

The following information relating to the balance sheet accounts at December 31 is obtained from supplementary records:

Notes receivable is a current asset.
The merchandise inventory is stated at cost by the LIFO method.
The product warranty payable is a current liability.
Vacation pay payable:
   Current liability $ 5,000
   Long-term liability   1,000
The unfunded pension liability is a long-term liability.
Notes payable:
   Current liability $115,000
   Long-term liability   335,000

6. On February 7 of the following year, the merchandise inventory was destroyed by fire. Based on the following data obtained from the accounting records, estimate the cost of the merchandise destroyed:

Jan. 1 Merchandise inventory	$ 40,250
Jan. 1–Feb. 7 Purchases (net)	235,250
Jan. 1–Feb. 7 Sales (net)	420,000
Estimated gross profit rate	40%

DOS Instructions

1. Load the General Ledger Software program (IA1).

2. Load the file **C-3** from the program disk.

3. Carefully key your name in the Student Name field.

4. Save the file with a file name of XXXC-3 (where XXX are your initials).

5. Key the journal entries in the General Journal.

6. Display the journal entries.

7. Make corrections to the journal entries, if necessary.

8. Display a trial balance.

9. Key the adjusting entries in the General Journal. Key **Adj.Ent.** in the Reference field.

10. Display the adjusting entries. Key **Adj.Ent.** in the Reference restriction field to display only the adjusting entries.

11. Use the **Save Accounting File** command to save your data file.

12. Perform period-end closing.

13. Display a post-closing trial balance.

14. Display a balance sheet.

15. Use the **Save As** command and save your data file with a file name of XXXC-3P (where XXX are your initials, C-3 represents the problem number, and P represents post closing).

16. On a separate sheet, estimate the following: On February 7 of the following year, the merchandise inventory was destroyed by fire. Based on the following data obtained from the accounting records, estimate the cost of the merchandise destroyed:

Jan. 1	Merchandise inventory	$40,250
Jan. 1–Feb. 7	Purchases (net)	$235,250
	Sales (net)	$420,000
Estimated gross profit rate		40%

Windows Instructions

To access Help, click on the Help button that appears in most windows.

1. Open the file **C-3**.

2. Carefully key your name in the User Name field.

3. Save the file with a file name of XXXC-3 (where XXX are your initials).

4. Key the journal entries in the General Journal.

5. Display the journal entries.

6. Make corrections to the journal entries, if necessary.

7. Display a trial balance.

8. Key the adjusting entries in the General Journal. Key **Adj.Ent.** in the Reference field.

9. Display the adjusting entries. Click on **Adj.Ent.** in the Reference drop-down list to display only the adjusting entries.

10. Click on the **Save** toolbar button to save your data file.

11. Generate and post the closing journal entries.

12. Display a post-closing trial balance.

13. Click on the **Save As** toolbar button to save your data file. Key a file name of XXXC-3P (where XXX are your initials, C-3 represents the problem number, and P represents post closing).

14. Display a balance sheet.

15. On a separate sheet, estimate the following: On February 7 of the following year, the merchandise inventory was destroyed by fire. Based on the following data obtained from the accounting records, estimate the cost of the merchandise destroyed:

Jan. 1	Merchandise inventory	$40,250
Jan. 1 - Feb. 7	Purchases (net)	$235,250
	Sales (net)	$420,000
Estimated gross profit rate		40%

Problem 12–3A
Selected stock transactions
Objectives 4, 5, 7

Robin Corporation sells and services pipe welding equipment in Texas. The following selected accounts appear in the ledger of Robin Corporation on January 1, 2000, the beginning of the current fiscal year:

110	Cash	$ 147,900
120	Accounts Receivable	98,950
140	Merchandise Inventory	1,881,650
141	Prepaid Insurance	64,650
142	Supplies	102,950
151	Equipment	1,600,000
152	Accumulated Depreciation—Equipment	109,600
153	Building	4,330,000
154	Accumulated Depreciation—Building	672,000
210	Accounts Payable	32,000
310	Preferred Stock, $100 par (12,500 shares issued)	1,250,000
330	Paid-In Capital in Excess of Par—Preferred Stock	112,500
340	Common Stock, $10 par (400,000 shares issued)	4,000,000
350	Paid-In Capital in Excess of Par—Common Stock	600,000
380	Retained Earnings	1,450,000

During the year, the corporation completed a number of transactions affecting the stockholders' equity. They are summarized as follows:

a. Purchased 20,000 shares of treasury common for $380,000.
b. Sold 5,000 shares of treasury common for $135,000.
c. Sold 3,000 shares of preferred 3% stock at $110.
d. Issued 50,000 shares of common stock at $32, receiving cash.
e. Sold 10,000 shares of treasury common for $170,000.
f. Declared cash dividends of $3 per share on preferred stock and $0.25 per share on common stock.
g. Paid the cash dividends.

Instructions

Journalize the entries to record the transactions. Identify each entry by letter.

DOS Instructions

1. Load the General Ledger Software program (IA1).

2. Load the file **12-3A** from the program disk.

3. Carefully key your name in the Student Name field.

4. Save the file with a file name of XXX12-3A (where XXX are your initials).

5. Key the journal entries in the General Journal. Key the letter for each entry in the **Reference** field.

6. Display the journal entries.

7. Make corrections to the journal entries, if necessary.

8. Display a balance sheet.

9. Save your data file.

Windows Instructions

To access Help, click on the Help button that appears in most windows.

1. Open the file **12-3A**.

2. Carefully key your name in the User Name field.

3. Save the file with a file name of XXX12-3A (where XXX are your initials).

4. Key the journal entries in the General Journal. Key the letter for each entry in the Reference field.

5. Display the journal entries.

6. Make corrections to the journal entries, if necessary.

7. Display a balance sheet.

8. Save your data file.

Problem 12–4A
Entries for selected corporate transactions
Objectives 4, 5, 7

GPS Enterprises Inc. produces aeronautical navigation equipment. The stockholders' equity accounts of GPS Enterprises Inc., with balances on January 1 of the current fiscal year, are as follows:

110	Cash	$122,000
120	Accounts Receivable	426,325
140	Merchandise Inventory	584,550
141	Prepaid Insurance	25,225
142	Supplies	21,945
151	Land	305,400
152	Equipment	660,400
153	Accumulated Depreciation—Equipment	112,095
210	Accounts Payable	357,500
211	Cash Dividends Payable	76,000
310	Common Stock, $10 stated value (80,000 shares issued)	800,000
320	Paid-In Capital in Excess of Stated Value—Common Stock	180,000
370	Retained Earnings	497,750
380	Treasury Stock (4,000 shares)	60,000
395	Income Summary	182,500

The following selected transactions occurred during the year:

Jan.   31. Paid cash dividends of $1 per share on the common stock. The dividend had been properly recorded when declared on December 28 of the preceding fiscal year for $76,000.

Mar.   7. Sold all of the treasury stock for $81,000.

May   5. Issued 10,000 shares of common stock for $210,000.

June 11. Received land from the Olinville City Council as a donation. The land had an estimated fair market value of $75,000.

July 30. Declared a 4% stock dividend on common stock, to be capitalized at the market price of the stock, which is $22 a share.

Aug. 27. Issued the certificates for the dividend declared on July 30.

Oct.   8. Purchased 2,000 shares of treasury stock for $42,500.

Dec. 20. Declared an $0.80-per-share dividend on common stock.
       31. Closed the credit balance of the income summary account, $182,500.
       31. Closed the two dividends accounts to Retained Earnings.

Instruction*p+1Xs

1. Enter the January 1 balances in T accounts for the stockholders' equity accounts listed. Also prepare T accounts for the following: Paid-In Capital from Sale of Treasury Stock; Donated Capital; Stock Dividends Distributable; Stock Dividends; Cash Dividends.
2. Journalize the entries to record the transactions, and post to the nine selected accounts.
3. Determine the total stockholders' equity on December 31.

DOS Instructions

1. Load the General Ledger Software program (IA1).

2. Load the file **12-4A** from the program disk.

3. Carefully key your name in the Student Name field.

4. Save the file with a file name of XXX12-4A (where XXX are your initials).

5. Key the journal entries in the General Journal.

6. Display the journal entries. Key a date range of 01/01/-- to 12/31/--.

7. Make corrections to the journal entries, if necessary.

8. Display a balance sheet. Verify that total stockholders' equity is $1,850,470.

9. Save your data file.

Windows Instructions

To access Help, click on the Help button that appears in most windows.

1. Open the file **12-4A**.

2. Carefully key your name in the User Name field.

3. Save the file with a file name of XXX12-4A (where XXX are your initials).

4. Key the journal entries in the General Journal.

5. Display the journal entries.

6. Make corrections to the journal entries, if necessary.

7. Display a balance sheet. Verify that total stockholders' equity is $1,850,470.

8. Save your data file.

Problem 12–5A
Entries for selected corporate transactions
Objectives 4, 5, 6, 7

The accounts and their balances in the ledger of Ocean Pacific Corporation on January 1 of the current year are as follows:

110	Cash	$345,610
120	Accounts Receivable	219,885
130	Merchandise Inventory	505,642
141	Prepaid Insurance	121,666
142	Office Supplies	23,203
152	Equipment	342,775
153	Accumulated Depreciation—Equipment	111,625
210	Accounts Payable	188,755
310	Common Stock	460,000
320	Paid-In Capital in Excess of Par—Common Stock	179,400
350	Retained Earnings	715,501
370	Treasury Stock	96,500

Ocean Pacific Corporation manufactures and distributes leisure clothing. Selected transactions completed by Ocean Pacific during the current fiscal year are as follows:

Jan. 2. Split the common stock 5 for 1 and reduced the par from $50 to $10 per share. After the split, there were 75,000 common shares outstanding.

Mar. 3. Declared semiannual dividends of $4 on 10,000 shares of preferred stock and $0.60 on the 75,000 shares of $10 par common stock to stockholders of record on March 28, payable on April 15.

Apr. 15. Paid the cash dividends.

30. Purchased 8,000 shares of the corporation's own common stock at $17, recording the stock at cost.

July 10. Sold 3,000 shares of treasury stock at $20, receiving cash.

23. Declared semiannual dividends of $4 on the preferred stock and $0.75 on the common stock (before the stock dividend). In addition, a 2% common stock dividend was declared on the common stock outstanding, to be capitalized at the fair market value of the common stock, which is estimated at $21.

Aug. 25. Paid the cash dividends and issued the certificates for the common stock dividend.

Instructions

Journalize the transactions.

DOS Instructions

1. Load the General Ledger Software program (IA1).

2. Load the file **12-5A** from the program disk.

3. Carefully key your name in the Student Name field.

4. Save the file with a file name of XXX12-5A (where XXX are your initials).

5. Key the journal entries in the General Journal.

6. Display the journal entries. Key a date range of 01/01/-- to 12/31/--.

7. Make corrections to the journal entries, if necessary.

8. Display a balance sheet.

9. Save your data file.

Windows Instructions

To access Help, click on the Help button that appears in most windows.

1. Open the file **12-5A**.

2. Carefully key your name in the User Name field.

3. Save the file with a file name of XXX12-5A (where XXX are your initials).

4. Key the journal entries in the General Journal.

5. Display the journal entries.

6. Make corrections to the journal entries, if necessary.

7. Display a balance sheet.

8. Save your data file.

Problem 12–3B
Selected stock transactions
Objectives 4, 5, 7

The following selected accounts appear in the ledger of KWR Environmental Corporation on July 1, 1999, the beginning of the current fiscal year:

110	Cash	$ 50,300
120	Accounts Receivable	602,200
140	Merchandise Inventory.................................	709,300
141	Prepaid Insurance.......................................	46,400
142	Supplies	85,000
151	Equipment...	915,900
152	Accumulated Depreciation—Equipment	69,000
210	Accounts Payable	835,100
310	Preferred Stock, $50 par (7,000 shares issued)	350,000
330	Paid-In Capital in Excess of Par—Preferred Stock	28,000
340	Common Stock, $20 par (25,000 shares issued).........	500,000
350	Paid-In Capital in Excess of Par—Common Stock	90,000
380	Retained Earnings	537,000

During the year, the corporation completed a number of transactions affecting the stockholders' equity. They are summarized as follows:

a. Issued 5,000 shares of common stock at $30, receiving cash.
b. Sold 1,000 shares of preferred 4% stock at $53.
c. Purchased 2,500 shares of treasury common for $60,000.
d. Sold 1,500 shares of treasury common for $45,000.
e. Sold 500 shares of treasury common for $11,500.
f. Declared cash dividends of $2 per share on preferred stock and $1 per share on common stock.
g. Paid the cash dividends.

Instructions

Journalize the entries to record the transactions. Identify each entry by letter.

DOS Instructions

1. Load the General Ledger Software program (IA1).

2. Load the file **12-3B** from the program disk.

3. Carefully key your name in the Student Name field.

4. Save the file with a file name of XXX12-3B (where XXX are your initials).

5. Key the journal entries in the General Journal. Key the letter for each entry in the Reference field.

6. Display the journal entries.

7. Make corrections to the journal entries, if necessary.

8. Display a balance sheet.

9. Save your data file.

Windows Instructions

To access Help, click on the Help button that appears in most windows.

1. Open the file **12-3B**.

2. Carefully key your name in the User Name field.

3. Save the file with a file name of XXX12-3B (where XXX are your initials).

4. Key the journal entries in the General Journal. Key the letter for each entry in the Reference field.

5. Display the journal entries.

6. Make corrections to the journal entries, if necessary.

7. Display a balance sheet.

8. Save your data file.

Problem 12–4B
Entries for selected corporate transactions
Objectives 4, 5, 7

Pittard Enterprises Inc. manufactures bathroom fixtures. The stockholders' equity accounts of Pittard Enterprises Inc., with balances on January 1 of the current fiscal year, are as follows:

110	Cash	$ 178,223
120	Accounts Receivable	385,900
130	Merchandise Inventory	809,800
141	Prepaid Insurance	72,260
142	Supplies	90,900
151	Land	636,400
152	Equipment	508,717
153	Accumulated Depreciation—Equipment	98,500
210	Accounts Payable	221,800
211	Cash Dividends Payable	47,500
310	Common Stock, $25 stated value (50,000 shares issued)	1,250,000
320	Paid-In Capital in Excess of Stated Value—Common Stock	250,000
370	Retained Earnings	725,000
380	Treasury Stock (2,500 shares, at cost)	80,000
395	Income Summary	169,400

The following selected transactions occurred during the year:

Jan. 20. Received land from the city as a donation. The land had an estimated fair market value of $150,000.

29. Paid cash dividends of $1 per share on the common stock. The dividend had been properly recorded when declared on December 30 of the preceding fiscal year for $47,500.

Mar. 3. Issued 6,000 shares of common stock for $240,000.

Apr. 1. Sold all of the treasury stock for $105,000.

July 1. Declared a 2% stock dividend on common stock, to be capitalized at the market price of the stock, which is $42 a share.

Aug. 11. Issued the certificates for the dividend declared on July 1.

Nov. 20. Purchased 2,500 shares of treasury stock for $90,000.

Dec. 21. Declared a $0.50-per-share dividend on common stock.

Dec. 31. Closed the credit balance of the income summary account, $169,400.

       31. Closed the two dividends accounts to Retained Earnings.

Instructions

1. Enter the January 1 balances in T accounts for the stockholders' equity accounts listed. Also prepare T accounts for the following: Paid-In Capital from Sale of Treasury Stock; Donated Capital; Stock Dividends Distributable; Stock Dividends; Cash Dividends.
2. Journalize the entries to record the transactions, and post to the nine selected accounts.
3. Determine the total stockholders' equity on December 31.

DOS Instructions

1. Load the General Ledger Software program (IA1).

2. Load the file **12-4B** from the program disk.

3. Carefully key your name in the Student Name field.

4. Save the file with a file name of XXX12-4B (where XXX are your initials).

5. Key the journal entries in the General Journal.

6. Display the journal entries. Key a date range of 01/01/-- to 12/31/--.

7. Make corrections to the journal entries, if necessary.

8. Display a balance sheet. Verify that total stockholders' equity is $2,692,090.

9. Save your data file.

Windows Instructions

To access Help, click on the Help button that appears in most windows.

1. Open the file **12-4B**.

2. Carefully key your name in the User Name field.

3. Save the file with a file name of XXX12-4B (where XXX are your initials).

4. Key the journal entries in the General Journal.

5. Display the journal entries. Key a start date of 01/01/-- and an end date of 12/31/--.

6. Make corrections to the journal entries, if necessary.

7. Display a balance sheet. Verify that total stockholders' equity is $2,692,090.

8. Save your data file.

Problem 12–5B
*Entries for selected corpo-
rate transactions*
Objectives 4, 5, 6, 7

The accounts and their balances in the ledger of CSB Boating Supply Corporation on January 1 of the current year are as follows:

110	Cash	$503,209
120	Accounts Receivable	174,564
130	Merchandise Inventory	561,812
141	Prepaid Insurance	65,235
142	Office Supplies	73,601
151	Land	447,221
152	Equipment	492,850
153	Accumulated Depreciation—Equipment	152,623
210	Accounts Payable	249,310
310	Common Stock	970,000
320	Paid-In Capital in Excess of Par—Common Stock	264,700
350	Retained Earnings	791,859
370	Treasury Stock	110,000

Selected transactions completed by CSB Boating Supply Corporation during the current fiscal year are as follows:

Jan. 9. Split the common stock 4 for 1 and reduced the par from $100 to $25 per share. After the split, there were 100,000 common shares outstanding.

Feb. 10. Purchased 5,000 shares of the corporation's own common stock at $38, recording the stock at cost.

May 1. Declared semiannual dividends of $3 on 5,000 shares of preferred stock and $0.80 on the common stock to stockholders of record on May 20, payable on July 15.

July 15. Paid the cash dividends.

Aug. 22. Sold 2,500 shares of treasury stock at $44, receiving cash.

Nov. 30. Declared semiannual dividends of $3 on the preferred stock and $0.90 on the common stock. In addition, a 2% common stock dividend was declared on the common stock outstanding. The fair market value of the common stock is estimated at $51.

Dec. 30. Paid the cash dividends and issued the certificates for the common stock dividend.

Instructions

Journalize the transactions.

DOS Instructions

1. Load the General Ledger Software program (IA1).

2. Load the file **12-5B** from the program disk.

3. Carefully key your name in the Student Name field.

4. Save the file with a file name of XXX12-5B (where XXX are your initials).

5. Key the journal entries in the General Journal.

6. Display the journal entries. Key a date range of 01/01/-- to 12/31/--.

7. Make corrections to the journal entries, if necessary.

8. Display a balance sheet.

9. Save your data file.

Windows Instructions

To access Help, click on the Help button that appears in most windows.

1. Open the file **12-5B**.

2. Carefully key your name in the User Name field.

3. Save the file with a file name of XXX12-5B (where XXX are your initials).

4. Key the journal entries in the General Journal.

5. Display the journal entries.

6. Make corrections to the journal entries, if necessary.

7. Display a balance sheet.

8. Save your data file.

Comprehensive Problem 4

Selected transactions completed by Stryker Products Inc. during the fiscal year ending July 31, 2000, were as follows:

a. Issued 10,000 shares of $25 par common stock at $45, receiving cash.

b. Issued 7,500 shares of $100 par preferred 8% stock at $120, receiving cash.

c. Issued $2,000,000 of 10-year, 10 1/2% bonds at an effective interest rate of 10%, with interest payable semiannually. Use the present value tables in Appendix A to determine the bond proceeds. Round to the nearest dollar.

d. Declared a dividend of $0.40 per share on common stock and $2 per share on preferred stock. On the date of record, 100,000 shares of common stock were outstanding, no treasury shares were held, and 15,000 shares of preferred stock were outstanding.

e. Paid the cash dividends declared in (d).

f. Redeemed $300,000 of 8-year, 12% bonds at 101. The balance in the bond premium account is $7,900 after the payment of interest and amortization of premium have been recorded. (Record only the redemption of the bonds payable.)

g. Purchased 3,000 shares of treasury common stock at $42 per share.

h. Declared a 5% stock dividend on common stock and a $2 cash dividend per share on preferred stock. On the date of declaration, the market value of the common stock was $41 per share. On the date of record, 100,000 shares of common stock had been issued, 3,000 shares of treasury common stock were held, and 15,000 shares of preferred stock had been issued.

i. Issued the stock certificates for the stock dividends declared in (h) and paid the cash dividends to the preferred stockholders.

j. Purchased $100,000 of Dilmore Inc. 10-year, 15% bonds, directly from the issuing company, for $97,000 plus accrued interest of $3,750.

k. Sold, at $48 per share, 2,000 shares of treasury common stock purchased in (g).

l. Recorded the payment of semiannual interest on the bonds issued in (c) and the amortization of the premium for six months. The amortization was determined using the straight-line method. (Round the amortization to the nearest dollar.)

m. Accrued interest for four months on the Dilmore Inc. bonds purchased in (j). Also recorded amortization of $100.

Instructions

1. Journalize the selected transactions.
2. After all of the transactions for the year ended July 31, 2000, had been posted (including the transactions recorded in (1) and all adjusting entries), the following data were selected from the records of Stryker Products Inc.:

Income statement data:

Advertising expense	$ 75,000
Cost of merchandise sold	3,850,000
Delivery expense	17,000
Depreciation expense—office equipment	13,100
Depreciation expense—store equipment	45,000
Gain on redemption of bonds	4,900
Income tax:	
Applicable to continuing operations	254,775
Applicable to loss from disposal of a	
segment of the business	21,100
Applicable to gain from redemption of bonds	1,000
Interest expense	101,884
Interest revenue	1,350
Loss from disposal of a segment of the business	80,500
Miscellaneous administrative expenses	1,600
Miscellaneous selling expenses	6,300
Office rent expense	25,000
Office salaries expense	85,000
Office supplies expense	5,300
Sales	5,100,000
Sales commissions	95,000
Sales salaries expense	180,000
Store supplies expense	9,500

Retained earnings and balance sheet data:

Accounts payable	$ 149,500
Accounts receivable	280,500
Accumulated depreciation—office equipment	835,250
Accumulated depreciation—store equipment	2,214,750
Allowance for doubtful accounts	21,500
Bonds payable, 10 1/2%, due 2010	2,000,000
Cash	125,500
Common stock, $25 par (400,000 shares authorized;	
104,850 shares outstanding)	2,621,250
Deferred income tax payable (current portion, $4,700)	25,700

Dividends:

Cash dividends for common stock	120,000
Cash dividends for preferred stock	105,000
Stock dividends for common stock	198,850
Dividends payable	30,000
Income tax payable	55,900
Interest receivable	5,000
Investment in Dilmore Inc. bonds (long-term)	97,100
Merchandise inventory (July 31, 2000), at lower of cost (fifo) or market	425,000
Notes receivable	77,500
Office equipment	2,410,100
Organization costs	55,000
Paid-in capital from sale of treasury stock	12,000
Paid-in capital in excess of par—common stock	325,000
Paid-in capital in excess of par—preferred stock	240,000
Preferred 8% stock, $100 par (30,000 shares authorized; 15,000 shares issued)	1,500,000
Premium on bonds payable	59,196
Prepaid expenses	15,900
Retained earnings, August 1, 1999	2,868,684
Store equipment	9,282,671
Treasury stock (1,000 shares of common stock at cost of $42 per share)	42,000

a. Prepare a multiple-step income statement for the year ended July 31, 2000, concluding with earnings per share. In computing earnings per share, assume that the average number of common shares outstanding was 100,000 and preferred dividends were $105,000. Round to nearest cent.

b. Prepare a retained earnings statement for the year ended July 31, 2000.

c. Prepare a balance sheet in report form as of July 31, 2000.

DOS Instructions

1. Load the General Ledger Software program (IA1).

2. Load the file **C-4** from the program disk.

3. Carefully key your name in the Student Name field.

4. Save the file with a file name of XXXC-4 (where XXX are your initials).

5. Key the journal entries in the General Journal. Key the letter for each entry in the Reference field.

6. Display the journal entries.

7. Make corrections to the journal entries, if necessary.

8. Display the income statement, balance sheet, and retained earnings statement.

9. Use the **Save Accounting File** command to save your data file.

10. Perform period-end closing.

11. Display a post-closing trial balance.

12. Use the **Save As** command and save your data file with a file name of XXXC-4P (where XXX are your initials, C-4 identifies the problem, and P indicates post-closing).

Windows Instructions

To access Help, click on the Help button that appears in most windows.

1. Open the file **C-4**.

2. Carefully key your name in the User Name field.

3. Save the file with a file name of XXXC-4 (where XXX are your initials).

4. Key the journal entries in the General Journal. Key the letter for each entry in the Reference field.

5. Display the journal entries.

6. Make corrections to the journal entries, if necessary.

7. Display the income statement, balance sheet, and retained earnings statement.

8. Click on the **Save** toolbar button to save your data file.

9. Generate and post the closing journal entries.

10. Display a post-closing trial balance.

11. Click on the **Save As** menu item in the File menu and save your data file with a file name of XXXC-4P (where XXX are your initials, C-4 identifies the problem, and P indicates post-closing.

Problem 15–4A
Statement of cash flows—
direct method
Objective 4

The comparative balance sheet of Corning Plumbing Supply Company for December 31, 2001 and 2000, is as follows:

	Dec. 31, 2001	Dec. 31, 2000
Assets		
Cash	$ 69,200	$ 76,500
Accounts receivable (net)	135,700	132,400
Inventories	223,800	201,400
Investments	—	45,000
Land	74,000	—
Equipment	340,000	250,000
Accumulated depreciation	(79,300)	(66,800)
	$763,400	$638,500
Liabilities and Stockholders' Equity		
Accounts payable (merchandise creditors)	$194,300	$187,400
Accrued expenses (operating expenses)	5,000	6,400
Dividends payable	3,800	3,000
Common stock, $1 par	14,000	10,000
Paid-in capital in excess of par—common stock	138,000	90,000
Retained earnings	408,300	341,700
	$763,400	$638,500

The income statement for the year ended December 31, 2001, is as follows:

Sales		$867,000
Cost of merchandise sold		553,000
Gross profit		$314,000
Operating expenses:		
Depreciation expense	$ 12,500	
Other operating expenses	198,000	
Total operating expenses		210,500
Operating income		$103,500
Other income:		
Gain on sale of investments		9,000
Income before income tax		$112,500
Income tax expense		28,000
Net income		$ 84,500

The following additional information was taken from the records:

a. Equipment and land were acquired for cash.
b. There were no disposals of equipment during the year.
c. The investments were sold for $54,000 cash.
d. The common stock was issued for cash.
e. There was a $17,900 debit to Retained Earnings for cash dividends declared.

Instructions

Prepare a statement of cash flows, using the direct method of presenting cash flows from operating activities.

DOS Instructions

1. Load the General Ledger Software program (IA1).

2. Load the file **15-4A** from the program disk.

3. Carefully key your name in the Student Name field.

4. Save the file with a file name of XXX15-4A (where XXX are your initials).

5. Choose **Financial Analysis** in the Reports menu and display a statement of cash flows.

6. Save your data file.

Windows Instructions

To access Help, click on the Help button that appears in most windows.

1. Open the file **15-4A**.

2. Carefully key your name in the User Name field.

3. Save the file with a file name of XXX15-4A (where XXX are your initials).

4. Click on the **Reports** toolbar button and click on **Financial Analysis**. Display a statement of cash flows.

5. Save your data file.

Problem 15–4B
*Statement of cash flows—
direct method*
Objective 4

The comparative balance sheet of Green Thumb Nursery Inc. for December 31, 2000 and 2001, is as follows:

	Dec. 31, 2001	Dec. 31, 2000
Assets		
Cash	$ 136,700	$147,300
Accounts receivable (net)	220,000	210,500
Inventories	276,200	254,700
Investments	—	60,000
Land	95,000	—
Equipment	575,000	450,000
Accumulated depreciation	(176,500)	(134,000)
	$1,126,400	$988,500
Liabilities and Stockholders' Equity		
Accounts payable (merchandise creditors)	$ 58,400	$ 55,000
Accrued expenses (operating expenses)	7,100	8,000
Dividends payable	16,000	14,500
Common stock, $1 par	30,000	25,000
Paid-in capital in excess of par—common stock	510,000	400,000
Retained earnings	504,900	486,000
	$1,126,400	$988,500

The income statement for the year ended December 31, 2001, is as follows:

Sales		$1,430,000
Cost of merchandise sold		845,000
Gross profit		$ 585,000
Operating expenses:		
Depreciation expense	$ 42,500	
Other operating expenses	345,000	
Total operating expenses		387,500
Operating income		$ 197,500
Other income:		
Gain on sale of investments		15,000
Income before income tax		$ 212,500
Income tax expense		84,000
Net income		$ 128,500

The following additional information was taken from the records:

a. Equipment and land were acquired for cash.
b. There were no disposals of equipment during the year.
c. The investments were sold for $75,000 cash.
d. The common stock was issued for cash.
e. There was a $109,600 debit to Retained Earnings for cash dividends declared.

Instructions

Prepare a statement of cash flows, using the direct method of presenting cash flows from operating activities.

DOS Instructions

1. Load the General Ledger Software program (IA1).
2. Load the file **15-4B** from the program disk.
3. Carefully key your name in the Student Name field.
4. Save the file with a file name of XXX15-4B (where XXX are your initials).
5. Choose **Financial Analysis** in the Reports menu and display a statement of cash flows.
6. Save your data file.

Windows Instructions

To access Help, click on the Help button that appears in most windows.

1. Open the file **15-4B**.
2. Carefully key your name in the User Name field.
3. Save the file with a file name of XXX15-4B (where XXX are your initials).
4. Click on the **Reports** toolbar button and click on **Financial Analysis**. Display a statement of cash flows.
5. Save your data file.

Problem 16–1A
Horizontal analysis for income statement
Objective 1

For 2000, Wang Company reported its most significant decline in net income in years. At the end of the year, Hai Wang, the president, is presented with the following condensed comparative income statement:

Wang Company
Comparative Income Statement
For the Years Ended December 31, 2000 and 1999

	2000	1999
Sales	$495,000	$450,000
Sales returns and allowances	5,000	2,000
Net sales	$490,000	$448,000
Cost of goods sold	312,000	260,000
Gross profit	$178,000	$188,000
Selling expenses	$ 84,000	$ 70,000
Administrative expenses	38,500	35,000
Total operating expenses	$122,500	$105,000
Income from operations	$ 55,500	$ 83,000
Other income	2,500	2,000
Income before income tax	$ 58,000	$ 85,000
Income tax expense	20,000	28,000
Net income	$ 38,000	$ 57,000

Instructions

1. Prepare a comparative income statement with horizontal analysis for the two-year period, using 1999 as the base year. Round to one digit after the decimal place.
2. To the extent the data permit, comment on the significant relationships revealed by the horizontal analysis prepared in (1).

DOS Instructions

1. Load the General Ledger Software program (IA1).

2. Load the file **16-1A** from the program disk.

3. Carefully key your name in the Student Name field.

4. Save the file with a file name of XXX16-1A (where XXX are your initials).

5. Choose **Financial Analysis** in the Reports menu and display an income statement horizontal analysis.

6. On a separate sheet, to the extent the data permit, comment on the significant relationships revealed by the horizontal analysis.

7. Save your data file.

Windows Instructions

To access Help, click on the Help button that appears in most windows.

1. Open the file **16-1A**.

2. Carefully key your name in the User Name field.

3. Save the file with a file name of XXX16-1A (where XXX are your initials).

4. Click on the **Reports** toolbar button and click on **Financial Analysis**. Display an income statement (horizontal analysis).

5. On a separate sheet, to the extent the data permit, comment on the significant relationships revealed by the horizontal analysis.

6. Save your data file.

Problem 16–2A
Vertical analysis for income statement
Objective 1

For 2000, Kasouski Company initiated a sales promotion campaign that included the expenditure of an additional $10,000 for advertising. At the end of the year, Leszek Kasouski, the president, is presented with the following condensed comparative income statement:

Kasouski Company
Comparative Income Statement
For the Years Ended December 31, 2000 and 1999

	2000	1999
Sales	$720,000	$650,000
Sales returns and allowances	20,000	15,000
Net sales	$700,000	$635,000
Cost of goods sold	290,000	270,000
Gross profit	$410,000	$365,000
Selling expenses	200,000	190,000
Administrative expenses	125,000	115,000
Total operating expenses	$325,000	$305,000
Income from operations	$ 85,000	$ 60,000
Other income	10,000	9,000
Income before income tax	$ 95,000	$ 69,000
Income tax expense	35,000	26,000
Net income	$ 60,000	$ 43,000

Instructions

1. Prepare a comparative income statement for the two-year period, presenting an analysis of each item in relationship to net sales for each of the years. Round to one digit after the decimal place.
2. To the extent the data permit, comment on the significant relationships revealed by the vertical analysis prepared in (1).

DOS Instructions

1. Load the General Ledger Software program (IA1).

2. Load the file **16-2A** from the program disk.

3. Carefully key your name in the Student Name field.

4. Save the file with a file name of XXX16-2A (where XXX are your initials).

5. Choose **Financial Analysis** in the Reports menu and display an income statement vertical analysis.

6. On a separate sheet, to the extent the data permit, comment on the significant relationships revealed by the vertical analysis.

7. Save your data file.

Windows Instructions

To access Help, click on the Help button that appears in most windows.

1. Open the file **16-2A**.

2. Carefully key your name in the User Name field.

3. Save the file with a file name of XXX16-2A (where XXX are your initials).

4. Click on the **Reports** toolbar button and click on **Financial Analysis**. Display an income statement (vertical analysis).

5. On a separate sheet, to the extent the data permit, comment on the significant relationships revealed by the vertical analysis.

6. Save your data file.

Problem 16–1B
Horizontal analysis for income statement
Objective 1

For 1999, Better Biscuit Company reported its most significant increase in net income in years. At the end of the year, John Newton, the president, is presented with the following condensed comparative income statement:

Better Biscuit Company
Comparative Income Statement
For the Years Ended December 31, 2000 and 1999

	2000	1999
Sales	$840,000	$700,000
Sales returns and allowances	5,000	5,000
Net sales	$835,000	$695,000
Cost of goods sold	450,000	400,000
Gross profit	$385,000	$295,000
Selling expenses	$115,000	$100,000
Administrative expenses	49,500	45,000
Total operating expenses	$164,500	$145,000
Income from operations	$220,500	$150,000
Other income	4,500	6,000
Income before income tax	$225,000	$156,000
Income tax expense	70,000	50,000
Net income	$155,000	$106,000

Instructions

1. Prepare a comparative income statement with horizontal analysis for the two-year period, using 1999 as the base year. Round to one digit after the decimal place.
2. To the extent the data permit, comment on the significant relationships revealed by the horizontal analysis prepared in (1).

DOS Instructions

1. Load the General Ledger Software program (IA1).

2. Load the file **16-1B** from the program disk.

3. Carefully key your name in the Student Name field.

4. Save the file with a file name of XXX16-1B (where XXX are your initials).

5. Choose **Financial Analysis** in the Reports menu and display an income statement horizontal analysis.

6. On a separate sheet, to the extent the data permit, comment on the significant relationships revealed by the horizontal analysis.

7. Save your data file.

Windows Instructions

To access Help, click on the Help button that appears in most windows.

1. Open the file **16-1B**.

2. Carefully key your name in the User Name field.

3. Save the file with a file name of XXX16-1B (where XXX are your initials).

4. Click on the **Reports** toolbar button and click on **Financial Analysis**. Display an income statement (horizontal analysis).

5. On a separate sheet, to the extent the data permit, comment on the significant relationships revealed by the horizontal analysis.

6. Save your data file.

Problem 16–2B
Vertical analysis for
income statement
Objective 1

For 2000, Stainless Exhaust Systems Inc. initiated a sales promotion campaign that included the expenditure of an additional $50,000 for advertising. At the end of the year, Edmundo Gonzalez, the president, is presented with the following condensed comparative income statement:

Stainless Exhaust Systems Inc.
Comparative Income Statement
For the Years Ended December 31, 2000 and 1999

	2000	1999
Sales	$490,000	$460,000
Sales returns and allowances	10,000	10,000
Net sales	$480,000	$450,000
Cost of goods sold	215,000	200,000
Gross profit	$265,000	$250,000
Selling expenses	$150,000	$100,000
Administrative expenses	85,000	80,000
Total operating expenses	$235,000	$180,000
Income from operations	$ 30,000	$ 70,000
Other income	10,000	9,000
Income before income tax	$ 40,000	$ 79,000
Income tax expense	14,000	30,000
Net income	$ 26,000	$ 49,000

Instructions

1. Prepare a comparative income statement for the two-year period, presenting an analysis of each item in relationship to net sales for each of the years. Round to one digit after the decimal place.
2. To the extent the data permit, comment on the significant relationships revealed by the vertical analysis prepared in (1).

DOS Instructions

1. Load the General Ledger Software program (IA1).

2. Load the file **16-2B** from the program disk.

3. Carefully key your name in the Student Name field.

4. Save the file with a file name of XXX16-2B (where XXX are your initials).

5. Choose **Financial Analysis** in the Reports menu and display an income statement vertical analysis.

6. On a separate sheet, to the extent the data permit, comment on the significant relationships revealed by the vertical analysis.

7. Save your data file.

Windows Instructions

To access Help, click on the Help button that appears in most windows.

1. Open the file **16-2B**.

2. Carefully key your name in the User Name field.

3. Save the file with a file name of XXX16-2B (where XXX are your initials).

4. Click on the **Reports** toolbar button and click on **Financial Analysis**. Display an income statement (vertical analysis).

5. On a separate sheet, to the extent the data permit, comment on the significant relationships revealed by the vertical analysis.

6. Save your data file.

Problem 17–3A
Entries and schedules for unfinished jobs and completed jobs
Objective 5

New Media Printing Company uses a job order cost system. The following data summarize the operations related to production for April, the first month of operations:

a. Materials purchased on account, $41,300.
b. Materials requisitioned and factory labor used:

Job	Materials	Factory Labor
No. 101	$5,740	$2,500
No. 102	4,250	1,940
No. 103	8,410	5,300
No. 104	2,460	1,140
No. 105	4,000	2,480
No. 106	5,570	3,250
For general factory use	2,400	1,580

c. Factory overhead costs incurred on account, $14,600.
d. Depreciation of machinery and equipment, $4,100.
e. The factory overhead rate is $25 per machine hour. Machine hours used:

Job	Machine Hours
No. 101	120
No. 102	105
No. 103	250
No. 104	70
No. 105	140
No. 106	165
Total	850

f. Jobs completed: 101, 102, 104, and 105.
g. Jobs were shipped and customers were billed as follows: Job 101, $15,100; Job 102, $10,200; Job 104, $6,500.

Instructions

1. Journalize the entries to record the summarized operations.
2. Post the appropriate entries to T accounts for Work in Process and Finished Goods, using the identifying letters as dates. Insert memorandum account balances as of the end of the month.
3. Prepare a schedule of unfinished jobs to support the balance in the work in process account.
4. Prepare a schedule of completed jobs on hand to support the balance in the finished goods account.

DOS Instructions

1. Load the General Ledger Software program (IA1).

2. Load the file **17-3A** from the program disk.

3. Carefully key your name in the Student Name field.

4. Save the file with a file name of XXX17-3A (where XXX are your initials).

5. Key the journal entries in the General Journal. Key the letter for each entry in the Reference field.

6. Display the journal entries.

7. Display a trial balance. Verify the Work in Process balance is $32,905.

8. Make corrections to the journal entries, if necessary.

9. On a separate sheet, complete instructions 2, 3, and 4.

10. Save your data file.

Windows Instructions

To access Help, click on the Help button that appears in most windows.

1. Open the file **17-3A**.

2. Carefully key your name in the User Name field.

3. Save the file with a file name of XXX17-3A (where XXX are your initials).

4. Key the journal entries in the General Journal. Key the letter for each entry in the Reference field.

5. Display the journal entries.

6. Display a trial balance. Verify the Work in Process balance is $32,905.

7. Make corrections to the journal entries, if necessary.

8. On a separate sheet, complete instructions 2, 3, and 4.

9. Save your data file.

Problem 17–3B
Entries and schedules for unfinished jobs and completed jobs
Objective 5

Hi Gloss Printing Company uses a job order cost system. The following data summarize the operations related to production for June, the first month of operations:

a. Materials purchased on account, $39,700.
b. Materials requisitioned and factory labor used:

Job	Materials	Factory Labor
No. 601	$9,470	$5,300
No. 602	3,260	1,890
No. 603	5,790	3,050
No. 604	2,450	1,240
No. 605	8,450	4,160
No. 606	4,380	2,540
For general factory use	2,500	1,600

c. Factory overhead costs incurred on account, $12,800.
d. Depreciation of machinery and equipment, $3,200.
e. The factory overhead rate is $20 per machine hour. Machine hours used:

Job	Machine Hours
No. 601	250
No. 602	105
No. 603	185
No. 604	85
No. 605	230
No. 606	160
Total	1,015

f. Jobs completed: 601, 602, 603, and 605.
g. Jobs were shipped and customers were billed as follows: Job 601, $25,000; Job 602, $11,400; Job 605, $19,800.

Instructions

1. Journalize the entries to record the summarized operations.
2. Post the appropriate entries to T accounts for Work in Process and Finished Goods, using the identifying letters as dates. Insert memorandum account balances as of the end of the month.
3. Prepare a schedule of unfinished jobs to support the balance in the work in process account.
4. Prepare a schedule of completed jobs on hand to support the balance in the finished goods account.

DOS Instructions

1. Load the General Ledger Software program (IA1).

2. Load the file **17-3B** from the program disk.

3. Carefully key your name in the Student Name field.

4. Save the file with a file name of XXX17-3B (where XXX are your initials).

5. Key the journal entries in the General Journal. Key the letter for each entry in the Reference field.

6. Display the journal entries.

7. Display a trial balance. Verify the Work in Process balance is $15,510.

8. Make corrections to the journal entries, if necessary.

9. On a separate sheet, complete instructions 2, 3, and 4.

10. Save your data file.

Windows Instructions

To access Help, click on the Help button that appears in most windows.

1. Open the file **17-3B**.

2. Carefully key your name in the User Name field.

3. Save the file with a file name of XXX17-3B (where XXX are your initials).

4. Key the journal entries in the General Journal. Key the letter for each entry in the Reference field.

5. Display the journal entries.

6. Display a trial balance. Verify the Work in Process balance is $15,510.

7. Make corrections to the journal entries, if necessary.

8. On a separate sheet, complete instructions 2, 3, and 4.

9. Save your data file.

Problem18–2A
Entries for process cost system
Objectives 2, 5

Thompson Container Company manufactures aluminum cans. Materials are placed in production in the Blanking Department and after processing are transferred to the Forming Department, where more materials (coatings) are added. The finished product emerges from the Forming Department.

The accounts and their balances in the ledger of Thompson Container Company on July 1 of the current year are as follows:

110	Cash	$ 74,989
120	Marketable Securities	34,000
130	Accounts Receivable	215,400
131	Allowance for Doubtful Accounts	36,000
140	Finished Goods—Aluminum Cans	125,000
143	Materials	35,400
150	Prepaid Expenses	12,800
160	Fixed Assets	981,600
161	Accumulated Depreciation—Fixed Assets	437,000
180	Patents	45,100
210	Accounts Payable	109,300
220	Wages Payable	19,400
230	Income Tax Payable	1,500
250	Mortgage Note Payable	94,000
260	Factory Overhead—Blanking	286
261	Factory Overhead—Forming	110
262	Maintenance and Repair	315
310	Common Stock	675,000
330	Retained Earnings	355,000
410	Sales	247,800
510	Cost of Goods Sold	178,600
610	Selling Expenses	150,900
620	Administrative Expenses	113,400
710	Interest Income	1,200
810	Interest Expense	400
910	Income Tax	7,900

There were no inventories of work in process at the beginning or at the end of July. Finished goods inventory at July 1 was 5,000 cases of aluminum cans at a total cost of $125,000.

Transactions related to manufacturing operations for July are summarized as follows:

a. Materials purchased on account, $134,000.
b. Materials requisitioned for use: Blanking, $98,300 ($93,400 entered directly into the product); Forming, $32,800 ($28,600 entered directly into the product).
c. Labor costs incurred: Blanking, $76,450 ($71,200 entered directly into the product); Forming, $102,700 ($92,300 entered directly into the product).
d. Miscellaneous costs and expenses incurred on account: Blanking, $11,400; Forming, $19,900.
e. Expiration of various prepaid expenses: Blanking, $3,600; Forming, $2,800.
f. Depreciation charged on fixed assets: Blanking, $32,000; Forming, $22,500.
g. Factory overhead applied to production, based on machine hours: $58,000 for Blanking and $60,000 for Forming.
h. Output of Blanking: 15,000 cases.
i. Output of Forming: 15,000 cases of aluminum cans.
j. Sales on account: 18,000 cases of aluminum cans at $40. Credits to the finished goods account are to be made according to the first-in, first-out method.

Instructions

Journalize the entries to record the transactions, identifying each by letter. Include as an explanation for entry (j) the number of cases and the cost per case of cans sold.

DOS Instructions

1. Load the General Ledger Software program (IA1).

2. Load the file **18-2A** from the program disk.

3. Carefully key your name in the Student Name field.

4. Save the file with a file name of XXX18-2A (where XXX are your initials).

5. Key the journal entries in the General Journal. Key the letter for each entry in the Reference field.

6. Display the journal entries.

7. Make corrections to the journal entries, if necessary.

8. Display the income statement, balance sheet, and retained earnings statement.

9. Save your data file.

Windows Instructions

To access Help, click on the Help button that appears in most windows.

1. Open the file **18-2A**.

2. Carefully key your name in the User Name field.

3. Save the file with a file name of XXX18-2A (where XXX are your initials).

4. Key the journal entries in the General Journal. Key the letter for each entry in the Reference field.

5. Display the journal entries.

6. Make corrections to the journal entries, if necessary.

7. Display the income statement, balance sheet, and retained earnings statement.

8. Save your data file.

Problem 18–2B
Entries for process cost system
Objectives 2, 5

Elf Bakery Inc. manufactures cookies. Materials are placed in production in the Baking Department and after processing are transferred to the Packing Department, where more materials are added. The finished products emerge from the Packing Department.

The accounts and their balances in the ledger of Elf Bakery Inc. on March 1 of the current year are as follows.

110	Cash	$ 83,000
120	Marketable Securities	36,000

130	Accounts Receivable	133,200
131	Allowance for Doubtful Accounts	38,000
140	Finished Goods	300,000
143	Materials	82,850
150	Prepaid Expenses	19,100
160	Fixed Assets	999,500
161	Accumulated Depreciation—Fixed Assets	557,000
180	Patents	37,180
210	Accounts Payable	188,100
220	Wages Payable	42,100
230	Income Tax Payable	2,100
250	Mortgage Note Payable	106,000
260	Factory Overhead—Baking	775
261	Factory Overhead—Packing	300
262	Maintenance and Repair	700
310	Common Stock	290,800
330	Retained Earnings	421,755
410	Sales	405,800
510	Cost of Goods Sold	180,400
610	Selling Expenses	89,900
620	Administrative Expenses	81,000
710	Interest Income	4,000
810	Interest Expense	850
910	Income Tax	10,900

There were no inventories of work in process at the beginning or at the end of March. Finished goods inventory at March 1 was 20,000 cases of cookies at a total cost of $300,000.

Transactions related to manufacturing operations for March are summarized as follows:

a. Materials purchased on account, $245,000.
b. Materials requisitioned for use: Baking Department, $191,500 ($185,000 entered directly into the product); Packing Department, $40,100 ($36,000 entered directly into the product).
c. Labor costs incurred: Baking Department, $81,200 ($78,000 entered directly into the product); Packing Department, $67,100 ($65,000 entered directly into the product).
d. Miscellaneous costs and expenses incurred on account: Baking Department, $16,800; Packing Department, $12,400.
e. Depreciation charged on fixed assets: Baking Department, $45,200; Packing Department, $12,400.
f. Expiration of various prepaid expenses: Baking Department, $4,300; Packing Department, $800.
g. Factory overhead applied to production, based on machine hours: $75,000 for Baking and $32,000 for Packing.
h. Output of Baking Department: 30,000 cases.
i. Output of Packing Department: 30,000 cases of cookies.
j. Sales on account: 40,000 cases of cookies at $25. Credits to the finished goods account are to be made according to the first-in, first-out method.

Instructions

Journalize the entries to record the transactions, identifying each by letter. Include as an explanation for entry (j) the number of cases and the cost per case of cookies sold.

DOS Instructions

1. Load the General Ledger Software program (IA1).

2. Load the file **18-2B** from the program disk.

3. Carefully key your name in the Student Name field.

4. Save the file with a file name of XXX18-2B (where XXX are your initials).

5. Key the journal entries in the General Journal. Key the letter for each entry in the Reference field.

6. Display the journal entries.

7. Make corrections to the journal entries, if necessary.

8. Display the income statement, balance sheet, and retained earnings statement.

9. Save your data file.

Windows Instructions

To access Help, click on the Help button that appears in most windows.

1. Open the file **18-2B**.

2. Carefully key your name in the User Name field.

3. Save the file with a file name of XXX18-2B (where XXX are your initials).

4. Key the journal entries in the General Journal. Key the letter for each entry in the Reference field.

5. Display the journal entries.

6. Make corrections to the journal entries, if necessary.

7. Display the income statement, balance sheet, and retained earnings statement.

8. Save your data file.

Exercise 20–3
*Static budget vs.
flexible budget*
Objectives 2, 4

The production supervisor of the Welding Department for Baxter Company agreed to the following monthly static budget for the upcoming year:

Baxter Company
Welding Department
Monthly Production Budget

Wages	$300,000
Utilities	160,000
Depreciation	50,000
Total	$510,000

The actual amount spent for the first three months of the year 2000 in the Welding Department was as follows:

January	$475,000
February	435,000
March	400,000

The Welding Department supervisor has been very pleased with this performance, since actual expenditures have been less than the monthly budget. However, the plant manager believes that the budget should not remain fixed for every month, but should "flex" or adjust to the volume of work that is produced in the Welding Department. Additional information for the Welding Department is as follows:

Wages per hour	$15.00
Utility cost per direct labor hour	$8.00
Direct labor hours per unit	0.40
Units produced	50,000

The actual units produced in the Welding Department were as follows:

January	45,000 units
February	40,000
March	35,000

a. Prepare a flexible budget for the actual units produced for January, February, and March in the Welding Department.
b. Compare the flexible budget with the actual expenditures for the first three months. What does this comparison suggest?

Windows Instructions   **To access Help, click on the Help button that appears in most windows.**

1. Open the file **20-3**.

2. Carefully key your name in the User Name field.

3. Save the file with a file name of XXX20-3 (where XXX are your initials).

4. Key the following journal entries in the General Journal to record the sales and production expenses for January, 2000. Key a date of 01/31/00 for each journal entry.

110	Cash	318,000	
410	Sales..		318,000
510	January Wages............................	276,000	
110	Cash		276,000
511	January Utilities..........................	149,000	
110	Cash		149,000
512	January Depreciation	50,000	
115	Accumulated Depreciation......		50,000

5. Display the journal entries.

6. Prepare a flexible budget for the actual units produced for January in the Welding Department.

7. Click on the **Other** toolbar button. Key your calculated budget figures for Wages, Utilities, and Depreciation for January in the Budget column. The sales budget has already been keyed for you. Click on the OK button.

8. Display the Budget Report.

   Click on the **Reports** toolbar button. Click on **Financial Statements**, **Budget Report**, and the OK button to choose a report to display. To print the report, click on the **Print** button.

9. Review the Budget Report and make any changes prior to Step 10.

10. Generate and post the closing journal entries.

11. Key the following journal entries in the General Journal to record the sales and production expenses for February, 2000. Key a date of 02/28/00 for each journal entry.

110	Cash	328,000	
410	Sales..		328,000
520	February Wages...........................	250,000	
110	Cash		250,000
521	February Utilities........................	135,000	
110	Cash		135,000
522	February Depreciation	50,000	
115	Accumulated Depreciation......		50,000

12. Display the journal entries. Click on the **Customize Journal Report** button and the OK button to display the journal entries for February.

13. Prepare a flexible budget for the actual units produced for February in the Welding Department.

14. Click on the **Other** toolbar button. Delete the amount of Total Revenue and the three January budget expense amounts. Key your calculated budget figures for Wages, Utilities, and Depreciation for February in the Budget column. Key $340,000 as the amount of Total Revenue for February. Click on the OK button.

15. Display the Budget Report.

   Click on the **Reports** toolbar button. Click on **Financial Statements**, **Budget Report**, and the OK button to choose a report to display. To print the report, click on the **Print** button.

16. Review the Budget Report and make any changes prior to Step 17.

17. Delete the closing journal entries in the General Journal.

    Click on the **Journal** toolbar button. Click on each Clo.Ent. journal entry. Click on the **Delete** button to delete the closing journal entry.

18. Generate and post the closing journal entries.

19. Key the following journal entries in the General Journal to record the sales and production expenses for March, 2000. Key a date of 03/31/00 for each journal entry.

110	Cash	322,000	
410	Sales..		322,000
530	March Wages..............................	230,000	
110	Cash		230,000
531	March Utilities...........................	120,000	
110	Cash		120,000
532	March Depreciation	50,000	
115	Accumulated Depreciation......		50,000

20. Display the journal entries. Click on the **Customize Journal Report** button and the OK button to display the journal entries for March.

21. Prepare a flexible budget for the actual units produced for March in the Welding Department.

22. Click on the **Other** toolbar button. Delete the amount of Total Revenue and the three February budget expense amounts. Key your calculated budget figures for Wages, Utilities, and Depreciation for March in the Budget column. Key $325,000 as the amount of Total Revenue for March.

23. Display the Budget Report.

    Click on the **Reports** toolbar button. Click on **Financial Statements**, **Budget Report**, and the OK button to choose a report to display. To print the report, click on the **Print** button.

24. Click on the **Save** toolbar button to save your data file.

Problem 21–4A
Standard factory overhead variance report
Objective 5

Health-Tex Company, a manufacturer of disposable medical supplies, prepared the following factory overhead cost budget for the Assembly Department for July of the current year. The company expected to operate the department at 100% of normal capacity of 6,000 hours.

Variable costs:		
Indirect factory wages	$15,000	
Power and light	4,800	
Indirect materials	6,600	
Total variable cost		$26,400
Fixed costs:		
Supervisory salaries	$24,400	
Depreciation of plant and equipment	6,400	
Insurance and property taxes	2,200	
Total fixed cost		33,000
Total factory overhead cost		$59,400

During July, the department operated at 4,500 hours, and the factory overhead costs incurred were: indirect factory wages, $10,990; power and light, $3,710; indirect materials, $4,910; supervisory salaries, $24,400; depreciation of plant and equipment, $6,400; and insurance and property taxes, $2,200.

Instructions

Prepare a factory overhead cost variance report for July. To be useful for cost control, the budgeted amounts should be based on 4,500 hours.

Windows Instructions

To access Help, click on the Help button that appears in most windows.

1. Open the file **21-4A.**

2. Carefully key your name in the User Name field.

3. Save the file with a file name of XXX21-4A (where XXX are your initials).

4. Calculate the budget for the factory overhead costs for July. The budgeted amounts should be based on 4,500 hours.

5. Click on the **Other** toolbar button. Key the budget amounts in the Budget column. The Sales budget has already been keyed for you. Click on the OK button

6. Display the Budget Report.

   Click on the **Reports** toolbar button. Click on **Financial Statements**, **Budget Report**, and the OK button to choose a report to display. To print the report, click on the **Print** button.

7. Click on the **Save** toolbar button to save your data file.

Problem 21–4B
Standard factory overhead variance report
Objective 5

Centipede, Inc., a manufacturer of construction equipment, prepared the following factory overhead cost budget for the Welding Department for May of the current year. The company expected to operate the department at 100% of normal capacity of 9,000 hours.

Variable costs:		
Indirect factory wages	$76,500	
Power and light	21,600	
Indirect materials	25,200	
Total variable cost		$123,300
Fixed costs:		
Supervisory salaries	$67,500	
Depreciation of plant and equipment	26,400	
Insurance and property taxes	5,100	
Total fixed cost		99,000
Total factory overhead cost		$222,300

During May, the department operated at 8,100 hours, and the factory overhead costs incurred were: indirect factory wages, $68,100; power and light, $19,950; indirect materials, $23,020; supervisory salaries, $67,500; depreciation of plant and equipment, $26,400; and insurance and property taxes, $5,100.

Instructions

Prepare a factory overhead cost variance report for May. To be useful for cost control, the budgeted amounts should be based on 8,100 hours.

Windows Instructions

To access Help, click on the Help button that appears in most windows.

1. Open the file **21-4B.**

2. Carefully key your name in the User Name field.

3. Save the file with a file name of XXX21-4B (where XXX are your initials).

4. Calculate the budget for the factory overhead costs for May. The budgeted amounts should be based on 9,000 hours.

5. Click on the **Other** toolbar button. Key the budget amounts in the Budget column. The Sales budget has already been keyed for you. Click on the OK button

6. Display the Budget Report.

   Click on the **Reports** toolbar button. Click on **Financial Statements**, **Budget Report**, and the OK button to choose a report to display. To print the report, click on the (s1p0s3b16901TPrint button.

7. Click on the **Save** toolbar button to save your data file.

Problem 22–1A
*Budget performance report
for a cost center*
Objective 2

The Reaction Department of the Gulf River Plant is organized as a cost center. The budget for the Reaction Department of the Gulf River Plant for the current month ended March 31 is as follows:

Factory wages	$245,000
Materials	346,000
Power and light	46,000
Supervisory salaries	54,000
Depreciation of plant and equipment	28,700
Maintenance	19,600
Insurance and property taxes	14,000
Total	$753,300

During March, the costs incurred in the Reaction Department were as follows:

Factory wages	$244,400
Materials	357,500
Power and light	47,700
Supervisory salaries	54,000
Depreciation of plant and equipment	28,700
Maintenance	19,300
Insurance and property taxes	14,000
Total	$765,600

Instructions

1. Prepare a budget performance report for the supervisor of the Reaction Department of the Gulf River Plant for the month of March.
2. For which costs might the supervisor be expected to request supplemental reports?

Windows Instructions

To access Help, click on the Help button that appears in most windows.

1. Open the file **22-1A.**

2. Carefully key your name in the User Name field.

3. Save the file with a file name of XXX22-1A (where XXX are your initials).

4. Prepare a budget performance report for the month of March.

5. Click on the **Other** toolbar button. Key the budget amounts in the Budget column. The Sales budget has already been keyed for you. Click on the OK button.

6. Display the Budget Report.

    Click on the **Reports** toolbar button. Click on **Financial Statements**, **Budget Report**, and the OK button to choose a report to display. To print the report, click on the **Print** button.

7. Click on the **Save** toolbar button to save your data file.

Problem 22–1B
*Budget performance report
for a cost center*
Objective 2

The Eastern District of Mobile Communications Inc. is organized as a cost center. The budget for the Eastern District of Mobile Communications Inc. for the current month ended September 30 is as follows:

Sales salaries	$ 735,000
Network administrat*p-1Xion salaries	410,000
Customer service salaries	145,000
Billing salaries	74,600
Maintenance	205,000
Depreciation of plant and equipment	174,600
Insurance and property taxes	24,200
Total	$1,768,400

During September, the costs incurred in the Eastern District were as follows:

Sales salaries	$ 747,900
Network administration salaries	408,300
Customer service salaries	163,600
Billing salaries	73,000
Maintenance	201,400
Depreciation of plant and equipment	174,600
Insurance and property taxes	24,200
Total	$1,793,000

Instructions

1. Prepare a budget performance report for the manager of the Eastern District of Mobile Communications Inc. for the month of September.
2. For which costs might the supervisor be expected to request supplemental reports?

Windows Instructions

To access Help, click on the Help button that appears in most windows.

1. Open the file **22-1B.**

2. Carefully key your name in the User Name field.

3. Save the file with a file name of XXX22-1B (where XXX are your initials).

4. Prepare a budget performance report for the month of September.

5. Click on the **Other** toolbar button. Key the budget amounts in the Budget column. The Sales budget has already been keyed for you. Click on the OK button.

6. Display the Budget Report.

    Click on the **Reports** toolbar button. Click on **Financial Statements**, **Budget Report**, and the OK button to choose a report to display. To print the report, click on the **Print** button.

7. Click on the **Save** toolbar button to save your data file.

Problem E–1
Foreign currency transactions

The accounts and their balances in the ledger of Global Inc. on January 1 of the current year are as follows:

110	Cash	$ 28,000
120	Notes Receivable	50,000
121	Accounts Receivable	53,340
130	Merchandise Inventory	80,000
141	Prepaid Insurance	3,140
142	Store Supplies	820
151	Store Equipment	154,200
152	Accumulated Depreciation—Store Equipment	93,900
210	Accounts Payable	33,000
211	Salaries Payable	2,700
212	Unearned Rent	3,800
310	Capital Stock	181,800
320	Retained Earnings	68,365
330	Cash Dividends	26,000
340	Income Summary	1,500
410	Sales	799,000
510	Cost of Goods Sold	474,300
610	Sales Salaries Expense	81,300
611	Advertising Expense	34,850
612	Depreciation Expense—Store Equipment	9,300
613	Store Supplies Expense	1,280
614	Miscellaneous Selling Expense	1,600
650	Office Salaries Expense	84,900
651	Rent Expense	45,000
652	Heating & Lighting Expense	37,400
653	Taxes Expense	7,850

654	Insurance Expense	1,060
655	Miscellaneous Administrative Expense	3,500
910	Income Tax	3,225

Global Inc. is a wholesaler of sports equipment, including golf clubs and gym sets. It sells to and purchases from companies in Canada and the Philippines. These transactions are settled in the foreign currency. The following selected transactions were completed during the current fiscal year:

June 10. Sold merchandise on account to Marco Company, net 30, 250,000 pesos; exchange rate, $0.030 per Philippines peso. The cost of merchandise sold was $5,500.

July 10. Received cash from Marco Company; exchange rate, $0.029 per Philippines peso.

15. Purchased merchandise on account from LeRa Inc., net 30, $5,000 Canadian; exchange rate, $0.76 per Canadian dollar.

Aug. 14. Issued check for amount owed to LeRa Inc.; exchange rate $0.75 per Canadian dollar.

31. Sold merchandise on account to Ramon Company, net 30, 100,000 pesos; exchange rate, $0.031 per Philippines peso. The cost of merchandise sold was $1,200.

Sept. 30. Received cash from Ramon Company; exchange rate, $0.032 per Philippines peso.

Oct. 8. Purchased merchandise on account from Chevalier Company, net 30, $50,000 Canadian; exchange rate, $0.73 per Canadian dollar.

Nov. 7. Issued check for amount owed to Chevalier Company; exchange rate, $0.74 per Canadian dollar.

Dec. 15. Sold merchandise on account to Jason Company, net 30, $80,000 Canadian; exchange rate, $0.75 per Canadian dollar. The cost of merchandise sold was $32,500.

16. Purchased merchandise on account from Juan Company, net 30, 500,000 pesos; exchange rate, $0.033 per Philippines peso.

31. Recorded unrealized currency exchange gain and/or loss on transactions of December 15 and 16. Exchange rates on December 31: $0.76 per Canadian dollar; $0.034 per Philippines peso.

Instructions

1. Journalize the entries to record the transactions and adjusting entries for the year, assuming that Global uses the perpetual inventory system.
2. Journalize the entries to record the payment of the December 16 purchase, on January 15, when the exchange rate was $0.031 per Philippines peso, and the receipt of cash from the December 15 sale, on January 17, when the exchange rate was $0.77 per Canadian dollar.

DOS Instructions

1. Load the General Ledger Software program (IA1).

2. Load the file **E-1** from the program disk.

3. Carefully key your name in the Student Name field.

4. Save the file with a file name of XXXE-1 (where XXX are your initials).

5. Key the journal entries for June through December 31 of the current year in the General Journal.

6. Key the journal entries for January 15 and January 17 of the following year in the General Journal.

7. Display the journal entries. Key a date range of 06/01/-- (where -- is the current year) and 01/31/-- (where -- is the following year).

8. Make corrections to the journal entries, if necessary.

9. Display the income statement, balance sheet, and retained earnings statement.

10. Use the **Save Accounting File** command to save your data file.

11. Perform period-end closing.

12. Display a post-closing trial balance.

13. Use the **Save As** command and save your data file with a file name of XXXE-1P (where XXX are your initials, E-1 represents the problem number, and P represents post closing).

Windows Instructions   **To access Help, click on the Help button that appears in most windows.**

1. Open the file **E-1**.

2. Carefully key your name in the User Name field.

3. Save the file with a file name of XXXE-1 (where XXX are your initials).

4. Key the journal entries for June through December 31 of the current year in the General Journal.

5. Key the journal entries for January 15 and January 17 of the following year in the General Journal.

6. Display the journal entries. Click on **Include All Journal Entries** and the OK button to display the journal entries.

7. Make corrections to the journal entries, if necessary.

8. Display the income statement, balance sheet, and retained earnings statement.

9. Click on the **Save** toolbar button to save your data file.

10. Generate and post the closing journal entries.

11. Display a post-closing trial balance.

12. Click on the **Save As** toolbar button and save your data file with a file name of XXXE-1P (where XXX are your initials, E-1 represents the problem number, and P represents post closing).

STUDENT REFERENCE GUIDE
FOR
DOS GENERAL LEDGER SOFTWARE

Opening Balances on the Data Disk

Your data disk contains the opening balances for several problems in your book. Each opening balance is identified with an icon in the margin.

START-UP INSTRUCTIONS

- **STEP 1** Start your computer.
- **STEP 2** At the DOS prompt, place your program disk in the disk drive.
- **STEP 3** Enter IA1.EXE to load the accounting program in the computer memory. If a problem uses depreciation, enter IA2.EXE to load the depreciation program.
- **STEP 4** The screen in Figure 1 will appear. Press Enter to select Yes to display the copyright information for this software. Select No if you do not want to read about the software.
  - **Note:** If the computer you are using has a mouse, click on the Yes button to display the copyright information. Click on the No button if you do not want to read about the software.

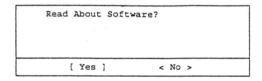

FIGURE 1 Opening Screen

- **STEP 5** If Yes was selected in the opening screen, Figure 2 will appear. If you are using a monochrome monitor and the screen image is unclear, choose MonoChrome to improve the image.

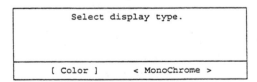

FIGURE 2 Select Display Type Screen

- **STEP 6** The first copyright screen will appear. The bottom line on the copyright screen shows the keys that are available now. You may use the up arrow and the down arrow keys to scroll through the displays. Use the PgUp, PgDn, Home, and End keys to move up and down one page and to the beginning and end of the copyright information. Press the F9 key to print the information. (See pages SR-8 through SR-9 for further information regarding the Print Options screen.) Press the Esc key to close this window.

- **STEP 7** After you have finished reading the copyright information, press the Esc key to close the window. An empty display screen will appear.

- **STEP 8** Press the Alt key to activate the menu bar.

- **STEP 9** When the reverse bar is on the File option, press Enter or press the down arrow key to display the File menu. You may also press the F key to pull down the File menu.

THE FILE MENU

The File Menu in Figure 3 provides access to the accounting file functions. It is the first menu you will select in order to open an existing file or create a new file. Other file functions in the File menu include saving, printing and erasing files. Exporting data to a spreadsheet file and exiting the Solutions Software is also done from the File menu.

To choose a command from the File menu, use the arrow keys to highlight the command and press Enter, or press the quick key (highlighted letter for each command). Notice that the F9 key is a hot key to print a report that is displayed.

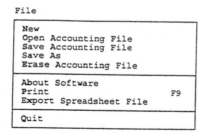

FIGURE 3 File Menu

New Accounting File

The New command on the File menu allows you to erase information from computer memory. Use the New command in Figure 4 to **create** an accounting file. If the New option is selected, a blank screen will appear. Additional general information is needed in order to enter data in the new file. This is done through the Options menu.

```
New
Open Accounting File
Save Accounting File
Save As
Erase Accounting File

About Solutions Software
Print                      F9
Export Spreadsheet File

Quit
```

FIGURE 4   New Accounting File

Open Accounting File

Use the Open Accounting File command to open (load from disk) an existing file. See Figure 5.

```
New
Open Accounting File
Save Accounting File
Save As
Erase Accounting File

About Solutions Software
Print                      F9
Export Spreadsheet File

Quit
```

FIGURE 5   Open Accounting File

A path and file name are required to open a file, as shown in Figure 6. The path field contains the disk drive and/or directory name where the file you wish to open is stored. The file name field contains the name of the file you wish to open. For example, the path and file shown in Figure 6 direct the computer to load file 01-5A from drive A.

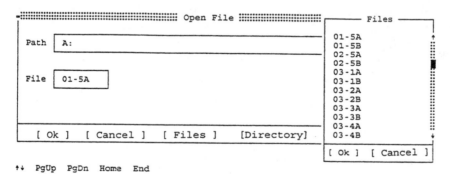

FIGURE 6   Path and File to Open Accounting File

To view a list of the accounting files in the specified directory, select the Directory button. To view the list of files, use the arrow keys or the PgUp and PgDn keys to move through the file list. Press the Home key to go to the top of the list. Press the End key to go to the bottom of the list. Press Enter to select the accounting file to open.

Select the Cancel button to exit from the Open Accounting File option without opening a file.

Save Accounting File

Use the Save Accounting File command to save your work-in-progress data to disk. See Figure 7. Your work-in-progress data will be saved under the **current** path and file name (as displayed in the upper right corner of the screen), overwriting the previous version of the file. This command can be selected at any time during the course of solving a problem.

```
New
Open Accounting File
Save Accounting File
Save As
Erase Accounting File

About Solutions Software
Print                        F9
Export Spreadsheet File

Quit
```

FIGURE 7   Save Accounting File

The software will not allow you to change an opening balances file and save it using the same name. An alert box will appear to let you know that opening balance files cannot be overwritten. See Figure 8. Select Ok to return to your accounting file and save the file using the Save As option, renaming the file using your initials. Instructions for saving and naming your file are included in the step-by-step instructions in each opening balances file.

```
        Cannot overwrite opening
             balances file.


                [ Ok ]
```

FIGURE 8   Alert Box

Save As

Use the Save As command to save your file under a **different** file name and/or path than the one currently displayed in the upper right corner of the screen. See Figure 9.

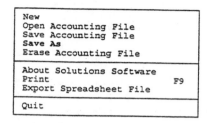

```
New
Open Accounting File
Save Accounting File
Save As
Erase Accounting File

About Solutions Software
Print                          F9
Export Spreadsheet File

Quit
```

FIGURE 9   Save As

Instructions for saving and naming your file are included in the step-by-step instructions in each opening balances file. Generally, your work will be saved using your initials and the problem number. See Figure 10 where the work on Problem 4-1A is saved in a file named XXX4-1A (where XXX are your initials). In addition, the Save As option is useful for making a backup. A backup is helpful if the original data disk is damaged or destroyed.

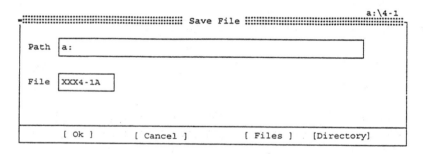

```
                                                          a:\4-1
::::::::::::::::::::::::::::::::::::::  Save File  ::::::::::::::::::::::::::::::::

   Path  | a:                                                    |

   File  | XXX4-1A |

         [ Ok ]        [ Cancel ]        [ Files ]    [Directory]
```

FIGURE 10   File Saved by Using Initials

Erase Accounting File

Use the Erase Accounting File command to remove a file from the directory. See Figure 11. If this option is selected, the file will be **permanently** removed from disk and cannot be restored.

A path and file name are required to erase a file, as shown in Figure 12. The path field contains the disk drive and/or directory name where the file you wish to erase is stored. The file name field contains the name of the file you wish to erase. For example, the path and file shown in Figure 12 direct the computer to erase the file XXX8-3A from Drive A.

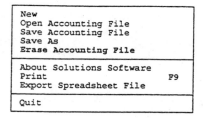

FIGURE 11 Erase Accounting File

To view a list of the accounting files in the specified directory, select the Directory button. Use the arrow keys or the PgUp and PgDn keys to move through the file list. Press the Home key to go to the top of the list. Press the End key to go to the bottom of the list. Press Enter to select the accounting file to erase.

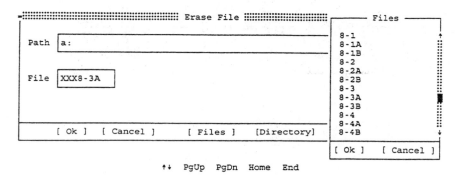

FIGURE 12 Erase Accounting File

If you select the Erase Accounting File option, an alert box will appear and you will be asked if you want to erase the file. See Figure 13. Double-check to be sure that the correct file name is displayed in the alert box before selecting the Ok button.

Select the Cancel button to exit from the Erase Accounting File option without erasing a file.

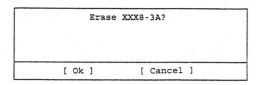

FIGURE 13 Alert Box

About Solutions Software

Use the About Software command to display copyright information for the software. See Figure 14.

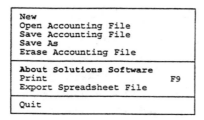
```
New
Open Accounting File
Save Accounting File
Save As
Erase Accounting File

About Solutions Software
Print                      F9
Export Spreadsheet File

Quit
```

FIGURE 14   About Solutions Software

Print

Use the Print command to print a report or copy a report to disk. See Figure 15. The report must be currently displayed on the screen before the Print option is selected. The F9 key is a hot key which may be used to print a report, without using the Print command from the File menu.

```
New
Open Accounting File
Save Accounting File
Save As
Erase Accounting File

About Solutions Software
Print                      F9
Export Spreadsheet File

Quit
```

FIGURE 15   Print

When Print is selected from the File menu, or the F9 key is pressed, the print options screen will appear. See Figure 16. Default settings have been preset. Generally, these settings will **not** need to be changed. If the default settings are correct, select the Ok button to print.

When the Each Report on a New Page option is set to Yes, each report will be printed on a new page. If the option is set to No, the computer will space down several lines and then continue to print on the same page, thus conserving paper.

The Number of Lines Per Page field represents the number of print lines that will fit on each page of paper. This option may be necessary for a printer that feeds individual sheets of paper.

If your computer has several printers attached, the Printed Output To option allows you to direct the output to a specific printer.

```
 ▪:::::::::::::::::::::::::::::::::::::::: Print Options :::::::::::::::::::::::::::::::::::::::::::::
   Each Report on a New Page:      Printed Output To:

      (♦) Yes                         (♦) LPT1
      ( ) No                          ( ) LPT2
                                      ( ) LPT3
   Number of Lines Per Page:  66      ( ) File: _____

                                      (♦) Append
                                      ( ) Replace

             [ Ok ]                              [ Cancel ]
```

FIGURE 16 Print Options to Print a Report

     To copy a report to a file, select the File option and key the drive and file name that is to receive the output in the box provided. Set the option buttons to indicate whether the output is to be added to the end of an existing file (Append) or a new file (Replace). Figure 17 shows the Print Options screen where the Trial Balance report has been selected to be copied to Drive A with a file name of 4-1.XXX (where 4-1 identifies the problem and XXX are your initials). In this case, the Trial Balance for Problem 4-1 is copied to a file on Drive A.

     There are many uses for a file containing a printed report. For example, it could be printed later with a DOS print command or with a word processor, or it could be merged into a word processing document.

     Press the Ok button to direct the computer to print the report. Once the report begins printing it may be stopped by pressing the Esc key. Press the Cancel button to exit the Print Options window.

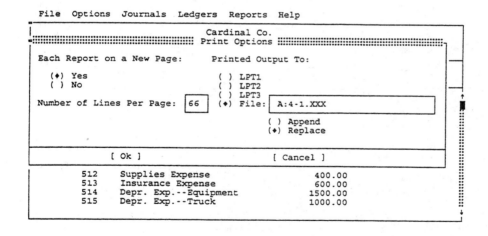

FIGURE 17 Print Options to Copy a Report to a File

Export Spreadsheet File

Use the Export Spreadsheet File command to export your data to a spreadsheet file. See Figure 18. The computer will create a spreadsheet file containing all active accounts and their respective account balances.

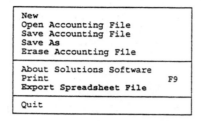

```
New
Open Accounting File
Save Accounting File
Save As
Erase Accounting File

About Solutions Software
Print                       F9
Export Spreadsheet File

Quit
```

FIGURE 18   Export Spreadsheet File

A path and file name are required to export a file, as shown in Figure 19. The path field contains the disk drive and/or directory name where the file you wish to export is stored. The file name field contains the name of the file you wish to export. Generally, the file name includes your initials and the problem name. The path and file shown in Figure 19 direct the computer to export data to a file named XXX9-6 on Drive A (where XXX are your initials and 9-6 identifies the problem). The computer will automatically give the file an extension of .wks to make the file compatible with most spreadsheet software.

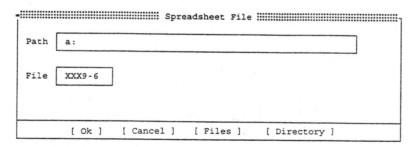

```
::::::::::::::::::::::::::::::::::::::: Spreadsheet File ::::::::::::::::::::::::::::::::::::::::::

   Path    a:

   File    XXX9-6

          [ Ok ]      [ Cancel ]      [ Files ]      [ Directory ]
```

FIGURE 19   Path and File for Export to Spreadsheet File

Quit

Use the Quit command when you are ready to end your session and exit Solutions Software. See Figure 20.

If changes were made to the file, save your work before quitting. If your data has not been saved, an alert box will appear advising that the file has not been saved. You will be asked if you want to save the data before quitting. See Figure 21.

```
New
Open Accounting File
Save Accounting File
Save As
Erase Accounting File

About Solutions Software
Print                      F9
Export Spreadsheet File

Quit
```

FIGURE 20   Quit

```
Warning!  Data file currently
stored in memory has not been
saved.  Do you wish to save
data first?

[ Yes ]      < No >       < Cancel >
```

FIGURE 21   Alert Box

THE OPTIONS MENU

The Options Menu in Figure 22 provides access to computer functions pertaining to the set up of accounting solution files, as well as computer functions relating to journal entries. Unless you are asked to set up a file where there are no existing opening balances, you will **not** need the set-up functions.

To choose a command from the Options menu, use the arrow keys to highlight the command and press Enter, or press the quick key (highlighted letter for each command).

```
Options

General Information
Required Accounts
Account Classification
Extended Classifications
Account Subtotals
Appropriation Accounts
Period-End Closing
Purge Journal Entries

Display Type
Set Colors
```

FIGURE 22   Options Menu

General Information

General Information contains important set-up information which is provided for each computerized accounting problem. Information includes Run Date, Company Name and Problem Name, as well as information pertaining to the business itself.

For each problem, you will be instructed to enter your name in the Student Name field and may be instructed to change the Run Date. The business organization, type of business, departmentalization, and accounting system buttons are preset when your data file is loaded. Select the Ok button to save your data. A General Information screen display is shown in Figure 23.

```
-:::::::::::::::::::::::::::::: General Information :::::::::::::::::::::::::::::::-
| Run Date...... 12/31/94                                                         |
| Student Name..                                                                  |
| Company Name.. Montrose Carpet Shop                                             |
| Problem Name.. 09-3A                                                            |
|---------------------------------------------------------------------------------|
| Business Organization:            Departmentalization:                          |
|    (♦) Sole Proprietorship           (♦) Not Departmentalized                   |
|    ( ) Partnership                   ( ) Two Departments                        |
|    ( ) Corporation                   ( ) Three Departments                      |
|                                                                                 |
| Type of Business:                 Accounting System:                            |
|    ( ) Service Business              ( ) Standard (Monthly Cycle)               |
|    (♦) Merchandising Business        (♦) Standard (Yearly Cycle)                |
|    ( ) Merch. Bus. with CGS Acct.    ( ) Voucher (Monthly Cycle)               |
|                                      ( ) Voucher (Yearly Cycle)                |
|---------------------------------------------------------------------------------|
|                   [ Ok ]              < Cancel >                                |
```

FIGURE 23   General Information Display

Required Accounts

Required Accounts contains important information which the computer requires in order to generate reports and prepare financial statements. You will not use this option when completing the assigned problems. A Required Accounts screen display is shown in Figure 24.

```
-:::::::::::::::::::::::::::::: Required Accounts :::::::::::::::::::::::::::::::-
| Acct. | Title                   | Required Accounts                          |
|-------|-------------------------|--------------------------------------------|
| 111   | Cash                    | Cash                                       |
| 112   | Accounts Receivable     | Accounts Receivable                        |
| 115   | Merchandise Inventory   | Merchandise Inventory                      |
|       |                         | Merchandise Inventory                      |
|       |                         | Merchandise Inventory                      |
| 211   | Accounts Payable        | Accounts/Vouchers Payable                  |
| 311   | George Montrose, Capital| Capital/Retained Earnings                  |
| 312   | George Montrose, Drawing| Drawing/Cash Dividends                     |
|       |                         | Stock Dividends                            |
| 313   | Income Summary          | Income Summary                             |
|       |                         | Income Summary                             |
|       |                         | Income Summary                             |
|-------|-------------------------|--------------------------------------------|
|                 [ Ok ]              < Cancel >                               |
```

FIGURE 24   Required Accounts Display

Account Classification

Account Classification contains important information which classifies accounts by type and range. This information is necessary for the computer to generate reports. You will not use this option when completing the assigned problems. An Account Classification screen display is shown in Figure 25.

```
-::::::::::::::: Account Classification :::::::::::::::::-
 ┌─────────────────────────┬─────────┬─────────┐
 │ Account Classification  │  From   │   To    │
 ├─────────────────────────┼─────────┼─────────┤
 │ Assets                  │  100    │  199    │
 │ Liabilities             │  200    │  299    │
 │ Capital/Equity          │  300    │  399    │
 │ Revenue                 │  400    │  499    │
 │ Cost                    │  500    │  599    │
 │ Expenses                │  600    │  699    │
 │ Other Revenue           │  700    │  799    │
 │ Other Expenses          │  800    │  899    │
 ├─────────────────────────┴─────────┴─────────┤
 │        [ Ok ]          < Cancel >           │
 └─────────────────────────────────────────────┘
```

FIGURE 25   Account Classification Display

Extended Classifications

Extended Classifications contains important information which identifies accounts by type and range. This information is necessary for the computer to generate the financial statement analyses. You will not use this option when completing the assigned problems. An Extended Classifications screen display is shown in Figure 26.

```
-::::::::::::: Extended Classification :::::::::::::::-
 ┌─────────────────────────┬─────────┬─────────┐
 │ Extended Classification │  From   │   To    │
 ├─────────────────────────┼─────────┼─────────┤
 │ Long-Term Assets        │  121    │  199    │
 │ Long-Term Liabilities   │  221    │  299    │
 │                         │         │         │
 │                         │         │         │
 │                         │         │         │
 │                         │         │         │
 ├─────────────────────────┴─────────┴─────────┤
 │        [ Ok ]          < Cancel >           │
 └─────────────────────────────────────────────┘
```

FIGURE 26   Extended Classification Display

Account Subtotals

Account Subtotals may contain information which identifies accounts by range. This information is necessary for the computer to generate reports containing subtotals. Not all problems will include Account Subtotals. You will not use this option when completing the assigned problems. An Account Subtotals screen display is shown in Figure 27.

```
:::::::::::::::::::::::::::::: Subtotals :::::::::::::::::::::::::::::
┌──────────┬──────────┬─────────────────────────────────────┐
│ From     │ To       │ Subtotal Title                      │
├──────────┼──────────┼─────────────────────────────────────┤
│ 111      │ 120      │ Total Current Assets                │
│ 121      │ 199      │ Total Plant Assets                  │
│ 600      │ 640      │ Total Selling Expenses              │
│ 641      │ 699      │ Total General Expenses              │
│          │          │                                     │
│          │          │                                     │
├──────────┴──────────┴─────────────────────────────────────┤
│          [ Ok ]          < Cancel >                        │
└────────────────────────────────────────────────────────────┘
```

FIGURE 27   Account Subtotals Display

Appropriation Accounts

Appropriation Accounts contains important information which identifies accounts which have been appropriated by a corporation. You will
not use this option when completing the assigned problems. An Appropriation Accounts screen display is shown in Figure 28.

```
::::::::::::::::::::::::::::: Appropriation Accounts :::::::::::::::::::::::::::::::
┌───────┬───────────────────────────┬──────────────────────────┐
│ Acct. │ Title                     │ Appropriation Accounts   │
├───────┼───────────────────────────┼──────────────────────────┤
│ 314   │ Appr. for Plant Expansion │ Appropriation Account    │
│ 315   │ Appr. for Bonded Indebted.│ Appropriation Account    │
│       │                           │ Appropriation Account    │
│       │                           │                          │
│       │                           │                          │
│       │                           │                          │
│       │                           │                          │
│       │                           │                          │
├───────┴───────────────────────────┼──────────────────────────┤
│          [ Ok ]                      < Cancel >               │
└────────────────────────────────────────────────────────────────┘
```

FIGURE 28   Appropriation Accounts Display

Period-End Closing

Perform the period-end closing at the end of each fiscal period. After
you select Period-End Closing, an alert box will appear asking you if
you want to perform the period-end closing. Select the Ok button to
perform the period-end closing. See Figure 29.

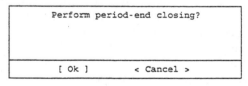

```
┌────────────────────────────────────────────────────┐
│           Perform period-end closing?                │
│                                                      │
│                                                      │
│                                                      │
├────────────────────────────────────────────────────┤
│        [ Ok ]            < Cancel >                  │
└────────────────────────────────────────────────────┘
```

FIGURE 29   Alert Box

As a result of period-end closing: (a) account balances are archived to previous year's balances; (b) all balances to the temporary income statement accounts are closed to the proper capital account(s); and (c) journal entries are erased.

Purge Journal Entries

Purge Journal Entries is used when the number of journal entries reaches the maximum capacity of 500. After selecting Purge Journal Entries, an alert box will appear asking you if you want to purge journal entries. See Figure 30. If you select the Ok button, all journal entries will be erased. You will not use this option when completing the assigned problems.

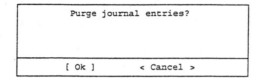

```
        Purge journal entries?




      [ Ok ]          < Cancel >
```

FIGURE 30   Alert Box

Display Type

Use the Display Type command to select the type of monitor you are using. If the screen image is unclear, choose MonoChrome to improve the image. See Figure 31.

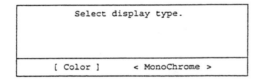

```
         Select display type.



      [ Color ]       < MonoChrome >
```

FIGURE 31   Select Display Type

Set Colors

If you have a color monitor, use the Set Colors command to change the color settings for menus, data entry windows and report windows. See Figure 32. The current default settings are displayed in three windows. Select the Change button to display the color choices. There are four sets of color choices. Select the Ok button to select the set of windows which you choose. Select the Cancel button to keep Set Colors at its current default setting.

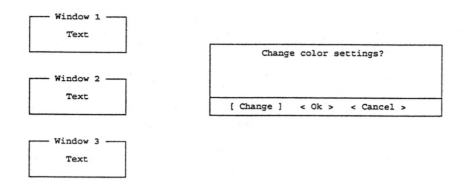

FIGURE 32   Set Colors Display

THE JOURNALS MENU

The Journals Menu in Figure 33 provides access to six journals. If a business uses a voucher system, a New Vouchers Journal would appear in the menu instead of the Purchases Journal.

To choose a journal from the Journals menu, use the arrow keys to highlight the journal and press Enter, or press the quick key (highlighted letter for each journal). To move between journals, press Shift-F1 through Shift-F5 simultaneously.

```
Journals
┌─────────────────────────────────┐
│ Opening Balances                │
├─────────────────────────────────┤
│ General Journal         S-F1    │
│ Purchases Journal       S-F2    │
│ Cash Payments Journal   S-F3    │
│ Sales Journal           S-F4    │
│ Cash Receipts Journal   S-F5    │
└─────────────────────────────────┘
```

FIGURE 33   Journals Menu

Opening Balances

Use the Opening Balances Journal to establish a new accounting file. Opening balances for accounts are keyed for a specific date. You will not need this journal when completing the assigned problems. Figure 34 shows an Opening Balances Journal.

```
.::::::::::::::::::::::::::::::::::::::::::::::::: Balances :::::::::::::::::::::::::::::::::::::::::::::::::::::::.
|                                                                                  |
|  Year....... 19--                                                                |
|  Date....... 12 / 31                                                             |
|  Reference.. Op. Bal.                   Proof In Balance                         |
|  +---------+-------+----------------------------+-----------+-----------+         |
|  | Acct.   | Ven./ |                            |           |           |         |
|  | No.     | Cus.  |  Account Title             |  Debit    | Credit    |         |
|  +---------+-------+----------------------------+-----------+-----------+         |
|  | 112     |       | Supplies                   |   675.00  |           |         |
|  | 113     |       | Prepaid Insurance          |  1950.00  |           |         |
|  | 116     |       | Accum. Depr.--Equipment    |  2100.00  |           |         |
|  | 512     |       | Salary Expense             | 15000.00  |           |         |
|  | 311     |       | Jan Dean, Capital          |           | 19725.00  |         |
|  |         |       |                            |           |           |         |
|  |         |       |                            |           |           |         |
|  +---------+-------+----------------------------+-----------+-----------+         |
|          [ Ok ]      < Cancel >      < Delete >                                   |
'----------------------------------------------------------------------------------'
```

FIGURE 34   Opening Balances Journal Display

General Journal

Use the General Journal to enter transactions for adjusting entries, reversing entries and entries which do not logically fit in any other journals.

For each transaction the sum of the debit entries must equal the sum of the credit entries. The computer adds the transactions as they are entered and displays a "Proof in Balance" message in the data entry window if the debit and credit amounts are equal. If not equal, the computer will display the amount of the difference and indicate if the difference is a debit or a credit. When entering transactions, enter the debit entry first. Figure 35 shows an adjusting entry in the General Journal.

```
  File  Options  Journals  Ledgers  Reports  Help
.:::::::::::::::::::::::::::::::::::: General Journal :::::::::::::::::::::::::::::::::::::::::.
|                                                                                  |
|  Year....... 19--                                                                |
|  Date....... 12 / 31                                                             |
|  Reference.. ADJ.ENT.                   Proof in Balance                         |
|  +---------+-------+----------------------------+-----------+-----------+         |
|  | Acct.   | Ven./ |                            |           |           |         |
|  | No.     | Cus.  |  Account Title             |  Debit    | Credit    |         |
|  +---------+-------+----------------------------+-----------+-----------+         |
|  | 514     |       | Supplies Expense           |   200.00  |           |         |
|  | 112     |       | Supplies                   |           |   200.00  |         |
|  |         |       |                            |           |           |         |
|  |         |       |                            |           |           |         |
|  |         |       |                            |           |           |         |
|  +---------+-------+----------------------------+-----------+-----------+         |
|       [ Ok ]       [ Cancel ]       [ List ]       [ Find ]                       |
'----------------------------------------------------------------------------------'
  F1=Chart  F4-F6=Accounts  Shft-F1 to Shft-F5=Journals
```

FIGURE 35   General Journal Display

To enter a transaction in the General Journal:

■ Key the date of the transaction.

■ Key descriptive information into the Reference field which will help identify the transaction; e.g., check number, invoice number. Key

Adj.Ent. or Rev.Ent. in the Reference field if the transaction is an adjusting or reversing entry. The Reference field may be left blank.

To record the debit and credit portions of the transaction, key the account number and debit or credit amounts.

■ If the account number is Accounts Receivable, key a customer number (if customers have been established as part of the problem). If the account number is Accounts Payable, key a vendor number (if vendors have been established as part of the problem).

■ Scroll boxes are available for the Chart of Accounts, Vendors and Customers by pressing the F1, F2 and F3 keys respectively.

■ Select the Ok button to obtain a Posting Summary. See Figure 36.

■ Select the Post button if the entry is correct or press the Change button if you need to return to the data entry window to make changes.

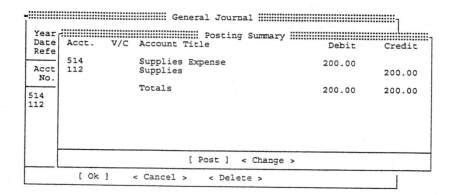

FIGURE 36   General Journal Posting Summary

To add a new account, vendor or customer:

■ Select either F4, F5 or F6 to display a list of the current Chart of Accounts, Vendors, or Customers.

■ Select Add New Account (New Vendor or New Customer).

■ Key the Acct. No. and Title of the new account (Vend. No. and Name or Cust. No. and Name).

■ The addition will be included in the current list.

Note: Press Shift-F1 through Shift-F5 simultaneously to move between the other journals and display the data entry windows for each journal.

Corrections to Journal Entries

To edit a journal entry, select the List button to display a list window of the transactions. Figure 37 shows a list of General Journal transactions. Use the arrow keys to highlight the transaction to be edited, then select the Ok button. Make the change(s) to the transaction in the data entry window. Select the Ok button to obtain a Posting Summary. Then select the Post button to post the entry if the data is correct.

```
┌───────────────────── Transactions ─────────────────────┐
 Date   Refer.   Acct.   V/C Title              Debit        Credit
 12/31  ADJ.ENT. 514         Supplies Expense    200.00
               112         Supplies                          200.00
 12/31  ADJ.ENT. 515         Insurance Expense   675.00
               113         Prepaid Insurance                 675.00
 12/31  ADJ.ENT. 516         Depr. Exp.--Equipment 800.00
               116         Accum. Depr.---Equipment          800.00
 12/31  ADJ.ENT. 512         Salary Expense      225.00
               212         Salaries Payable                  225.00



[ Ok ]                                              < Cancel >
```

FIGURE 37 Corrections to Journal Entries

To search for a journal entry, select the Find button and key into the Find What? field the data you are looking for. If the search is successful, the computer will display the entry in the data entry window for correction or deletion. If the entry is not found, the computer will display Not Found. The computer will **not** search for an account title. Figure 38 shows the Find What? window in a search for a transaction in the amount of $200.00.

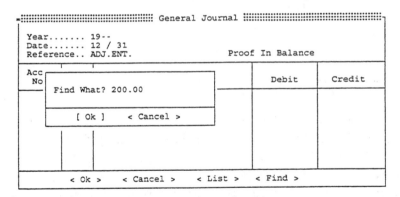

FIGURE 38 Find What? Display

Purchases Journal

Use the Purchases Journal to enter transactions for purchases made on account. To record entries in the Purchases Journal, key data into the fields in the top portion of the data entry window. Then make the debit entry or entries to complete the transaction. The computer automatically makes the entry for Accounts Payable Credit. Figure 39 shows an entry in the Purchases Journal.

For businesses using a voucher accounting system, the New Vouchers Journal will be used instead of the Purchases Journal and transactions will be entered using the same process as the Purchases Journal.

The function keys at the bottom of the data entry window work in the same manner as previously described for the General Journal.

```
File  Options  Journals  Ledgers  Reports  Help

▪::::::::::::::::::::::::::::: Purchases :::::::::::::::::::::::::::::::::::
 Year.................... 19--
 Date.................... 06 / 10
 Vendor Number.......... 210 Alamogordo Co.
 Invoice Number......... 214
 Invoice Amount.........    1019.50

 Accounts Payable Credit    1019.50
                    ──General Accounts──
 Acct.  │        Title              │  Debit
 ───────┼───────────────────────────┼──────────
 511    │ Purchases                 │  950.00
 512    │ Freight-In                │   69.50
        │                           │
        │                           │
 ───────┴───────────────────────────┴──────────
      < Ok >     < Cancel >    < List >    < Find >

F1=Chart  F2=Vendors  F4-F6=Accounts  Shft-F1 to Shft-F5=Journals
```

FIGURE 39 Purchases Journal

Cash Payments Journal

The Cash Payments Journal is used to enter transactions for all cash disbursements. To record entries in the Cash Payments Journal, key data into the fields in the top portion of the data entry window. Then make the debit entry or entries to complete the transaction. If the transaction involves a purchases discount, the credit to Purchases Discounts is recorded as a negative number in the debit column. The computer automatically makes the entry for Cash Credit. Figure 40 shows an entry in the Cash Payments Journal.

The function keys at the bottom of the data entry window work in the same manner as previously described for the General Journal.

```
File  Options  Journals  Ledgers  Reports  Help
┌──────────────── Cash Payments ──────────────────┐
│ Year................... 19--                     │
│ Date................... 02 / 03                  │
│ Vendor Number.......... 230 Best Equipment Co.   │
│ Check Number........... 103                      │
│ Accts. Pay. Debit ......   2500.00               │
│                                                  │
│ Cash Credit.............   2450.00               │
│              ──────General Accounts──────        │
│  Acct.  │       Title          │      Debit      │
│  511.2  │ Purchases Discounts   │      -50.00     │
│         │                       │                 │
│         │                       │                 │
│         │                       │                 │
│      < Ok >    < Cancel >    < List >    < Find > │
└──────────────────────────────────────────────────┘
   F1=Chart  F2=Vendors  F4-F6=Accounts  Shft-F1 to Shft-F5=Journals
```

FIGURE 40   Cash Payments Journal

Sales Journal

Use the Sales Journal to enter transactions for sales made on account. Key data into the fields in the top portion of the data entry window. Then make the credit entry or entries to complete the transaction. The computer automatically makes the entry for Accounts Receivable Debit. Figure 41 shows an entry in the Sales Journal.

The function keys at the bottom of the data entry window work in the same manner as previously described for the General Journal.

```
File  Options  Journals  Ledgers  Reports  Help
┌──────────────────── Sales ──────────────────────┐
│ Year................... 19--                     │
│ Date................... 12 / 31                  │
│ Customer No............ 120 Jane Cote            │
│ Invoice No............. 8                        │
│ Invoice Amount.........    259.70                │
│                                                  │
│ Accts. Receivable Debit    259.70                │
│              ──────General Accounts──────        │
│  Acct.  │       Title          │      Credit     │
│  411    │ Sales                 │      245.00     │
│  212    │ Sales Tax Payable     │       14.70     │
│         │                       │                 │
│         │                       │                 │
│      < Ok >    < Cancel >    < List >  < Find >   │
└──────────────────────────────────────────────────┘
   F1=Chart  F3=Customers  F4-F6=Accounts  Shft-F1 to Shft-F5=Journals
```

FIGURE 41   Sales Journal

Cash Receipts Journal

Use the Cash Receipts Journal to enter transactions for all cash receipts. Key data into the fields in the top half of the data entry window. Then make the credit entry or entries to complete the transaction. The computer automatically makes the entry for Cash Debit. Figure 42 shows an entry in the Cash Receipts Journal.

The function keys at the bottom of the data entry window work in the same manner as previously described for the General Journal.

```
File  Options  Journals  Ledgers  Reports  Help
▄▄▄▄▄▄▄▄▄▄▄▄▄▄▄▄▄▄▄▄▄▄▄ Cash Receipts ▄▄▄▄▄▄▄▄▄▄▄▄▄▄▄▄▄▄▄▄▄▄▄▄
    Year...................... 19--
    Date...................... 10 / 10
    Customer No............... 110 Adams Co.
    Reference.................
    Accts. Receivable Credit    3600.00

    Cash Debit................   3528.00
    ┌─────────────────General Accounts───────────────────────┐
    │ Acct. │          Title          │        Credit        │
    ├───────┼─────────────────────────┼──────────────────────┤
    │ 411.2 │ Sales Discounts         │         -72.00       │
    │       │                         │                      │
    │       │                         │                      │
    │       │                         │                      │
    │       │                         │                      │
    ├───────┴─────────────────────────┴──────────────────────┤
    │   < Ok >     < Cancel >    < List >    < Find >         │
    └─────────────────────────────────────────────────────────┘

F1=Chart F2=Vendors F3=Customers F4-F6=Accounts Shft-F1 to Shft-F5=Journals
```

FIGURE 42   Cash Receipts Journal

THE LEDGERS MENU

The Ledgers Menu in Figure 43 provides access to the Chart of Accounts, Vendors List, and Customers List. Data may be added, edited and/or deleted in these ledgers through the Maintain screens.

To choose a command from the Ledgers menu, use the arrow keys to highlight the command and press Enter, or press the quick key (highlighted letter for each command). Use the hot keys (F1 through F6) to select ledger commands without using the Ledgers pull down menu.

Move through the scroll boxes by using the arrow keys or the PgUp and PgDn keys. Select the Home key to go to the top of the scroll box. Select the End key to go to the bottom of the scroll box.

```
Ledgers

Chart of Accounts        F1
Vendor List              F2
Customer List            F3

Maintain Accounts        F4
Maintain Vendors         F5
Maintain Customers       F6
```

FIGURE 43   Ledgers Menu

Chart of Accounts

Select Chart of Accounts to display a scroll box of the current Chart of
Accounts. To select an account from the scroll box for entry into a data
entry window, highlight the account and select the Ok button. Figure 44
shows the Chart of Accounts in a scroll box.

```
─────────── Chart of Accounts ───────────
111    Cash                                    ↑
112    Accounts Receivable                     ▓
113    Store Supplies                          ▓
114    Office Supplies                         ▓
115    Merchandise Inventory                   ▓
117    Store Equipment                         ▓
117.1  Accum. Depr.--Store Eqpt.               ▓
118    Office Equipment                        ▓
118.1  Accum. Depr.--Ofc. Eqpt.                ▓
211    Accounts Payable                        ▓
212    Sales Tax Payable                       ▓
213    Salaries Payable                        ↓

[ Ok ]                         < Cancel >
```

FIGURE 44   Chart of Accounts Display

Vendor List

Select Vendor List to display a scroll box of the current vendors. To select a vendor from the scroll box for entry into a data entry window,
highlight the vendor and select the Ok button. Figure 45 shows the vendors in a scroll box.

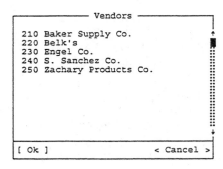

```
──────────── Vendors ────────────
210 Baker Supply Co.                 ↑
220 Belk's                           ▓
230 Engel Co.                        ▓
240 S. Sanchez Co.                   ▓
250 Zachary Products Co.             ▓
                                     ▓
                                     ▓
                                     ▓
                                     ▓
                                     ▓
                                     ▓
                                     ↓

[ Ok ]                   < Cancel >
```

FIGURE 45   Vendors List Display

Customer List

Select Customer List to display a scroll box of customers. To select a customer from the scroll box for entry into a data entry window, highlight the customer and select the Ok button. Figure 46 shows the customers in a scroll box.

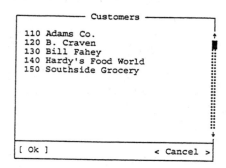

FIGURE 46   Customers List Display

Maintain Accounts

Use the Maintain Accounts command to add, edit or delete an account. See Figure 47. To add a new account, select —Add New Account— from the Chart of Accounts scroll box. Key the Acct. No. and Title. Select the Ok button.

To edit an account, highlight the account to edit. Select the Ok button, then make the changes in the list window. Select the Ok button. To delete an account, highlight the account to delete. Select the Ok button, then select the Delete button. An alert box will appear asking if you would like to delete the entry. Select the Ok button. The account balance must be zero before an account can be deleted.

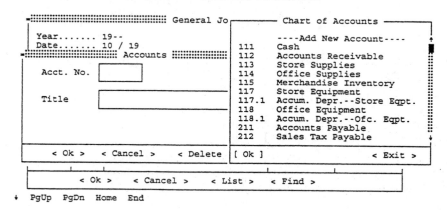

FIGURE 47   Maintain Accounts Display

Maintain Vendors

Use the Maintain Vendors command to add, edit or delete a vendor. See Figure 48. To add a new vendor, select —Add New Vendor— from the Vendors scroll box. Key the Vend. No. and Name. Select the Ok button.

 To edit a vendor, highlight the vendor to edit. Select the Ok button, then make the changes in the list window. Select the Ok button.

 To delete a vendor, highlight the vendor to delete. Select the Ok button, then select the Delete button. An alert box will appear asking if you would like to delete the entry. Select the Ok button. The vendor account balance must be zero before a vendor can be deleted.

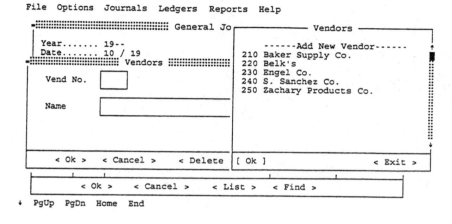

FIGURE 48 Maintain Vendors Display

Maintain Customers

Use the Maintain Customers command to add, edit or delete a customer. See Figure 49. To add a customer, select —Add New Customer— from the Customer scroll box. Key the Cust. No. and Name. Select the Ok button.

 To edit a customer, highlight the customer to edit. Select the Ok button, then make the changes in the list window. Select the Ok button.

 To delete a customer, highlight the customer to delete. Select the Ok button, then select the Delete button. An alert box will appear asking if you would like to delete the entry. Select the Ok button. The customer account balance must be zero before a customer can be deleted.

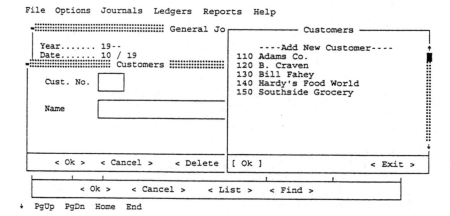

File Options Journals Ledgers Reports Help

```
::::::::::::::::::::::::::: General Jo┌──────── Customers ────────┐
 Year.......  19--                    │    ----Add New Customer----  ↑
 Date.......  10 / 19                 │ 110 Adams Co.                │
::::::::::::::::::::::::: Customers :::│ 120 B. Craven                │
                                      │ 130 Bill Fahey               │
  Cust. No.  ┌──────┐                 │ 140 Hardy's Food World       │
             └──────┘                 │ 150 Southside Grocery        │
                                      │                              │
  Name       ┌──────────────┐         │                              │
             └──────────────┘         │                              │
                                      │                              ↓
├──────────────────────────────────── ┼──────────────────────────────┤
│  < Ok >    < Cancel >    < Delete > │ [ Ok ]              < Exit > │
└──────────────────────────────────── └──────────────────────────────┘
      ┌────────────────────────────────────────────────────────┐
      │   < Ok >    < Cancel >    < List >    < Find >          │
      └────────────────────────────────────────────────────────┘
```
↓ PgUp PgDn Home End

FIGURE 49   Maintain Customers Display

THE REPORTS MENU

The Reports Menu in Figure 50 provides access to reports which are
generated by the computer. The reports may be displayed and printed.

   To choose a report from the Reports menu, use the arrow keys to
highlight the report and press Enter, or press the quick key (highlighted
letter for each journal).

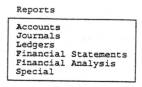

Reports

```
┌────────────────────────┐
│ Accounts               │
│ Journals               │
│ Ledgers                │
│ Financial Statements   │
│ Financial Analysis     │
│ Special                │
└────────────────────────┘
```

FIGURE 50   Reports Menu

Accounts

Select Accounts from the Reports menu to display a report selection
window for the Chart of Accounts, Vendor List, and Customer List.
Then press the space bar to place an X in the box next to the account(s)
you want to display. To display the report(s), select the Ok button. After
the report is displayed, press the F9 key to print the report. Figure 51
shows the Report Selection window for Accounts.

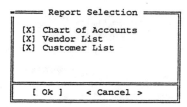

```
========== Report Selection ==========
  [X]  Chart of Accounts
  [X]  Vendor List
  [X]  Customer List


     [ Ok ]      < Cancel >
```

FIGURE 51   Report Selection for Accounts

Journals

Select Journals from the Reports menu to display a report selection window for the six journals. Then press the space bar to place an X in the box next to the journal(s) you want to display. To display the report(s), select the Ok button. After the report is displayed, press the F9 key to print the report. Figure 52 shows the Report Selection window for Journals where three journals have been selected for display.

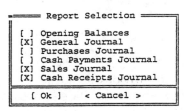

```
========== Report Selection ==========
  [ ]  Opening Balances
  [X]  General Journal
  [ ]  Purchases Journal
  [ ]  Cash Payments Journal
  [X]  Sales Journal
  [X]  Cash Receipts Journal
     [ Ok ]      < Cancel >
```

FIGURE 52   Report Selection for Journals

Enter the date range of the transactions you want to include in the report and add a reference restriction, if appropriate. For example, Adj.Ent. would be entered in the Reference restriction area if the report you want to display is for adjusting entries only. Figure 53 shows the Selection Options for journal entries dated 10/01/94 through 10/31/94 with a Reference restriction of Adj.Ent.

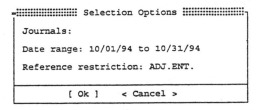

```
========== Selection Options ==========
  Journals:

  Date range: 10/01/94 to 10/31/94

  Reference restriction: ADJ.ENT.

     [ Ok ]      < Cancel >
```

FIGURE 53   Selection Options for Journals

Ledgers

Select Ledgers from the Reports menu to display a report selection window for the six ledgers. Then press the space bar to place an X in the box next to the ledger(s) you want to display. To display the report(s), select the Ok button. After the report is displayed, press the F9 key to print the report. Figure 54 shows the Report Selection window for ledgers where three ledgers have been selected for display.

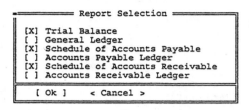

FIGURE 54 Report Selection for Ledgers

Financial Statements

Select Financial Statements from the Reports menu to display a report selection window for the Income Statement, Balance Sheet, and Statement of Owner's Equity (or Retained Earnings Statement). Then press the space bar to place an X in the box next to the financial statement(s) you want to display. To display the report(s), select the Ok button. When the report is displayed, press the F9 key to print the report. Figure 55 shows the Report Selection window for financial statements where all the financial statements have been selected for display.

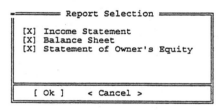

FIGURE 55 Report Selection for Financial Statements

Financial Analysis

Select Financial Analysis from the Reports menu to display a report selection window for the five financial analysis reports. Then press the space bar to place an X in the box next to the financial analysis reports you want to display. To display the report(s), select the Ok button. When the report is displayed, press the F9 key to print the report. Figure 56 shows the Report Selection window for financial analysis reports where all financial analysis reports have been selected for display.

```
╔════════════ Report Selection ════════════╗
║                                           ║
║  [X]  Statement of Cash Flows             ║
║  [X]  Income Stmt. Horizontal Analysis    ║
║  [X]  Income Stmt. Vertical Analysis      ║
║  [X]  Balance Sheet Horizontal Analysis   ║
║  [X]  Balance Sheet Vertical Analysis     ║
║                                           ║
╠═══════════════════════════════════════════╣
║        [ Ok ]      < Cancel >             ║
╚═══════════════════════════════════════════╝
```

FIGURE 56   Report Selection for Financial Analysis

Special

Select Special from the Reports menu to access the report selection window for Checks and Statements. This option is available only for a voucher system. If the accounting system is a standard system and not a voucher system as indicated in the General Information data entry window, the Special command will be dimmed and you will not be able to access this feature.

To display Checks and/or Statements, press the space bar to place an X in the box next to Checks and/or Statements. Figure 57 shows the Report Selection window where Checks and Statements have been selected.

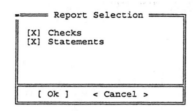

FIGURE 57   Report Selection for Special

If Checks is selected for display, enter the date range of the transactions you want to include in the report. Assign the Beginning Check Number. Press the Ok button. When the Checks are displayed, press the F9 key if you want to print the checks. Figure 58 shows the Selection Options window for checks.

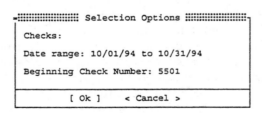

FIGURE 58   Selection Options for Checks

If Statements is selected, enter the Customer number range. Select the Ok button. When the Statements are displayed, press the F9 key if you want to print the statements. Figure 59 shows the Selection Options window for statements.

```
-:::::::::::::::::: Selection Options :::::::::::::::::::-
|                                                        |
| Statements:                                            |
|                                                        |
| Customer number range:                                 |
|                                                        |
| 110 to 150                                             |
|                                                        |
|--------------------------------------------------------|
|              [ Ok ]      < Cancel >                     |
```

FIGURE 59 Selection Options for Statements

THE HELP MENU

The Help Menu in Figure 60 provides access to additional information regarding how to operate the software. Select the area for which help is needed. Press the F9 key to print the information.

To choose a command from the Help menu, use the arrow keys to highlight the command and press Enter, or press the quick key (highlighted letter) for each command.

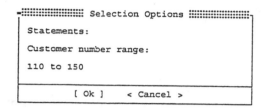

```
Help

Pull Down Menus
Data Entry Windows
Alert Boxes
Scroll Boxes
Printing Reports
```

FIGURE 60 Help Menu

Pull Down Menus

The menu bar contains six menu items, each with its own pull down menu. Each of the menus and menu items can be accessed, by using your keyboard or a mouse, unless the menu or menu item is dimmed. When a menu or menu item is dimmed, the software will not permit access to the menu or menu item.

The Journals menu contains hot keys (S-F1 to S-F5) which identify Journals. The hot keys can be used to move between journals when you are in journal data entry windows. The File menu contains a hot key (F9) which can be used to print a report while the report is displayed on the screen. The Ledgers menu contains hot keys (F1 to F6) to provide quick access to the Ledger menu commands.

Using the Keyboard to Select Pull Down Menus:

■ Press the Alt key to activate the menu bar. Each menu will appear with its quick key letter highlighted, colored or underlined.

■ Choose the menu you want by moving the cursor to the desired menu (use the arrow keys) and pressing Enter, or by pressing the appropriate quick key letter. To select a menu item, highlight the item using the arrow keys and press Enter, or press the appropriate quick key.

Using the Mouse to Select Pull Down Menus

■ Click on the menu you would like to pull down from the menu bar.

■ Click on the menu item you choose.

Figure 61 shows the information contained in the Help menu regarding Menu Selection using the mouse and the keyboard.

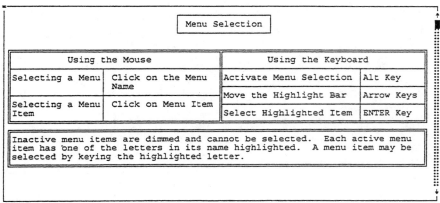

F9=Print Esc=Close Window

FIGURE 61 Help for Menu Selection

Data Entry Windows

Data should be keyed into the data entry windows from left-to-right and top-to-bottom. Buttons at the bottom of the data entry windows allow you to accept or cancel the data inputted. Use the quick keys at the bottom of the window for quick access to the Ledger commands (F1 to F6) and to move between journals (S-F1 to S-F5).

Using the Keyboard for Data Entry:

■ Move between fields using the Tab key. This is known as normal tab sequence. Press Shift-Tab simultaneously to move backwards through the fields.

- Pull down menus from the menu bar may be displayed while the data entry windows are displayed.
- Press Ctrl-Enter simultaneously or select the Ok button to save your data.
- Press Esc to remove a data entry window display.

Using the Mouse for Data Entry:
- Click on the field where data is to be entered.
- Click on the Ok button to accept the data entry window.
- Click on the Cancel button to erase the data entered.
- Click on the = in the upper left corner to close the window.

Figure 62 shows the information included in the Help menu regarding Data Entry Windows using the mouse and the keyboard.

Using the Mouse		Using the Keyboard	
Select a Field	Click on the Field	Next Field	Tab / ENTER
		Previous Field	Shift-Tab
Select a Button	Click on the Button	Select Highlighted Button	Ctrl-ENTER
		Move to Top of Window	Home
Close Current Window	Click on the = in upper left corner.	Move to Bottom of Window	End
		Move Down One Field	Down Arrow
		Move Up One Field	Up Arrow
Move Window	Point to Title Bar and drag window.	Move Cursor to Right	Right Arrow
		Move Cursor to Left	Left Arrow
		Cursor to Begin of Field	Ctrl-Home
		Cursor to End of Field	Ctrl-End
Function Keys		Blank a Field	+
		Toggle Insert/Overstrike	Insert
Menu items relevent to the current data entry screen may be selected via the appropriate function keys displayed near the bottom of the screen.		Destructive BackSpace	Backspace
		Delete a Character	Delete
		Activate Button Option	Space Bar
		Close Current Window	Esc

↑↓ PgUp PgDn Home End F9=Print Esc=Close Window

FIGURE 62   Help for Data Entry Windows

Alert Boxes

Alert boxes appear on the display screen that provide informational and error messages while operating the software. When these boxes appear, one of the actions shown must be selected before other work can proceed.

Using the Keyboard to Respond to Alert Boxes:
- Press the Tab key until the desired button is activated.
- Press the Enter key to perform the specified action.

Using the Mouse to Respond to Alert Boxes:
- Position the cursor on the desired button.
- Click the mouse to perform the specified action.

Figure 63 shows the information included in the Help file regarding Alert Boxes using the mouse and the keyboard.

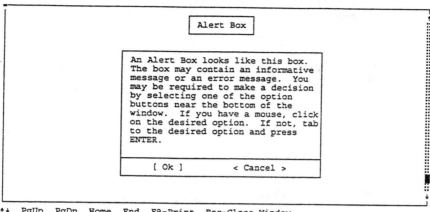

```
                    ┌──────────────┐
                    │   Alert Box  │
                    └──────────────┘

            ┌─────────────────────────────────┐
            │ An Alert Box looks like this box.│
            │ The box may contain an informative│
            │ message or an error message.  You │
            │ may be required to make a decision│
            │ by selecting one of the option    │
            │ buttons near the bottom of the    │
            │ window.  If you have a mouse, click│
            │ on the desired option.  If not, tab│
            │ to the desired option and press    │
            │ ENTER.                             │
            │                                    │
            ├─────────────────────────────────┤
            │   [ Ok ]          < Cancel >       │
            └─────────────────────────────────┘
```

↑↓ PgUp PgDn Home End F9=Print Esc=Close Window

FIGURE 63 Help for Alert Boxes

Scroll Boxes

Scroll boxes are list windows where data are displayed. These boxes provide information that can be used in other windows. The list windows can be scrolled from top to bottom.

Using the Keyboard with Scroll Boxes:

■ Press the up arrow key and down arrow key to scroll one line at a time.

■ Press the PgUp and PgDn keys to scroll one page at a time.

■ Press the End key to scroll to the end of the list.

■ Press the Home key to scroll to the beginning of the list.

■ Use the up arrow key or down arrow key to position the highlight bar on the desired item and press Enter to select the item.

Using the Mouse with Scroll Boxes:

■ To scroll up one line at a time, click on the up arrow icon located at the top of the scroll bar to position the highlight bar on the desired item.

■ To scroll down one line at a time, click on the down arrow icon located at the bottom of the scroll bar to position the highlight bar on the desired item.

■ To scroll up one page at a time, position the cursor immediately below the scroll box and click the mouse.

■ To scroll down one page at a time, position the cursor immediately above the scroll box and click the mouse.

■ To scroll up rapidly, position the cursor on the up arrow icon, then click-and-hold the mouse button down. Or, position the cursor immediately below the last item in the list, then click-and-hold the mouse button down.

■ To scroll down rapidly, position the cursor on the down arrow icon, then click-and-hold the mouse button down. Or, position the cursor immediately above the first item in the list, then click-and-hold the mouse button down.

Figure 64 shows the information included in the Help file regarding Scroll Boxes using the mouse and the keyboard.

```
┌────────────────────────────────────────────────────────────────┐↑
│                        ┌──────────────┐                          ┊
│                        │  Scroll Box  │                          ┊
│                        └──────────────┘                          ┊
│  ┌──────────────────────────────┬─────────────────────────────┐ ┊
│  │       Using the Mouse        │     Using the Keyboard       │ ┊
│  ├────────────┬─────────────────┼──────────────────┬──────────┤ ┊
│  │ Scroll Up  │ Click on the ↑  │ Scroll Up        │ Up Arrow │ ┊
│  │            │                 │ Scroll Down      │Down Arrow│ ┊
│  │ Scroll Down│ Click on the ↓  │ Scroll Up One Page│ Page Up │ ┊
│  │            │                 │ Scroll Down One Page│Page Down│┊
│  │ Page Up    │ Click on the scroll│Highlight First Entry│ Home │┊
│  │            │ bar ▦ above the │ Highlight Last Entry│ End    │ ┊
│  │            │ scroll box ▮    │ Highlight Next Button│ Tab   │ ┊
│  │            │                 │Highlight Previous Button│Shift-Tab│┊
│  │ Page Down  │ Click on the scroll│Select Highlighted Button│ENTER│▮
│  │            │ bar ▦ below the │ Cancel Scroll Box │ Esc    │  ┊
│  │            │ scroll box ▮    │                  │          │ ┊
│  │ Scroll to a│ Drag the scroll │                  │          │ ┊
│  │ Point in Window│ box ▮       │                  │          │ ┊
│  │ Select a Button│ Click on the Button│           │          │ ┊
│  └────────────┴─────────────────┴──────────────────┴──────────┘ ┊
└──────────────────────────────────────────────────────────────────┘
```

FIGURE 64 Help for Scroll Boxes

Printing Reports

Report selection windows are used to select computer generated reports for display. One or more reports may be selected at a time in the report selection windows. The reports may also be printed.

Using the Keyboard to Tag Reports to be Displayed:

■ Press the Tab key to position the cursor in the appropriate box.

■ Press the space bar to place an X inside the box for each report you want to display. (Press the space bar again to remove the X from the box if you decide not to display the report.)

■ Press the Tab key to move the cursor to the Ok button, then press Enter (or press the Ctrl-Enter keys simultaneously) to accept the report selection window.

Using the Mouse to Tag Reports to be Displayed:

■ Click on each report you want to display to place an X inside the box. (A second click on the report will remove the X if you decide not to display the report.)

■ Click on the Ok button.

Figure 65 shows the information included in the Help file regarding Printing Reports.

```
                          ┌─────────────────┐
                          │ Printing Reports │
                          └─────────────────┘
┌───────────────────────────────────────────────────────────────────┐
│  1.  Select the desired report from the Reports menu.               │
│                                                                     │
│  2.  While the report is displayed in the report display box, pull  │
│      down the File menu and select the Print option, or press the   │
│      F9 key.                                                        │
│                                                                     │
│  3.  TO PRINT A REPORT, review the default settings in the Report   │
│      Options window and make any changes necessary.                 │
│                                                                     │
│  4.  Select the Ok button to print the report.                      │
│                                                                     │
│  5.  TO COPY A REPORT TO DISK, select File in the Report Options    │
│      window and key a file name in the box provided.                │
│                                                                     │
│  6.  Select Append to send more than one report to a file with the  │
│      same name or select Replace to send one report to a file.      │
│                                                                     │
│  7.  Select the Ok button to copy the report to a file.             │
│                                                                     │
└───────────────────────────────────────────────────────────────────┘
```

FIGURE 65   Help for Printing Reports